Gershom G. Scholem

תרנ"ח — תשמ"ב 1897 — 1982

Gershom Scholem: The Man and His Work

SUNY Series in Judaica:
Hermeneutics, Mysticism, and Religion

Michael Fishbane, Robert Goldenberg, and Elliot Wolfson, Editors

Gershom Scholem
The Man and His Work

edited by

Paul Mendes-Flohr

STATE UNIVERSITY OF NEW YORK PRESS
THE ISRAEL ACADEMY OF SCIENCES AND HUMANITIES

The articles by E. Urbach ('Gershom Scholem and Judaic Studies'), J. Ben-Shlomo ('Gershom Scholem on Pantheism in the Kabbala'), I. Tishby ('Gershom Scholem's Contribution to the Study of the Zohar'), R. Schatz ('Gershom Scholem's Interpretation of Hasidism as an Expression of His Idealism'), M. Beit-Arié ('Gershom Scholem as Bibliophile') and N. Rotenstreich ('Gershom Scholem's Conception of Jewish Nationalism') originally appeared in Hebrew in *Gershom Scholem — 'Al ha-'ish u-fo'alo*, © The Israel Academy of Sciences and Humanities, 1983.

The poem by Gershom Scholem on pp. 17–19 was originally published in German in *Walter Benjamin/Gershom Scholem Briefwechsel 1933–1940*, © 1980 by Suhrkamp Verlag, Frankfurt a/M, and appeared in English translation in W. Benjamin and G. Scholem, *The Correspondence of Walter Benjamin and Gershom Scholem*, © 1989 by Schocken Books, Inc. It is reprinted here by permission of Suhrkamp Verlag and by permission of Schocken Books, Inc., published by Pantheon Books, a division of Random House, Inc.

Published by State University of New York Press, Albany, and The Israel Academy of Sciences and Humanities, Jerusalem

© 1994 by The Israel Academy of Sciences and Humanities

Printed in the United States of America
Set by Crispin, Jerusalem

For information, address State University of New York Press,
State University Plaza, Albany, N.Y. 12246

Production by Marilyn P. Semerad
Marketing by Fran Keneston

Library of Congress Cataloging-in-Publication Data

Gershom Shalom,'al ha-ish u-fo' olo. English.
    Gershom Scholem: the man and his work/editedby Paul Mendes
-Flohr.
        p. cm. — (SUNY series in Judaica)
    Includes bibliographical references.
    ISBN 0-7914-2125-2. — ISBN 0-7914-2126-0 (pbk.)
    1. Scholem, Gershom Gerhard, 1897- —Congresses. 2. Jewish
scholars—Israel—Biography—Congresses. 3. Mysticism—Judaism-
-Historiography—Congresses. I. Scholem, Gershom Gerhard, 1897-
. II. Mendes-Flohr, Paul R. III. Title. IV. Series.
BM755. S295G4713 1944
296´ .092—dc20
(B)   93-47893
                                                                              CIP

10 9 8 7 6 5 4 3 2 1

296.092
S368

IN MEMORIAM

Three of the authors represented in this volume have passed away since the original Hebrew publication of their contributions.

Rivka Schatz-Uffenheimer (1927–1992) was born in Lodz, Poland, and raised in Sao Paulo, Brazil. After earning her doctorate on 'quietistic elements' in hasidic mysticism under the supervision of Gershom Scholem at the Hebrew University of Jerusalem, she went on to teach Kabbala and Hasidism there and to publish extensively on Hasidism and on the typology of messianic thought. She laid the groundwork for a critical edition of the *Zohar*, sponsored by the Israel Academy of Sciences and Humanities; the edifice, sadly, will have to be completed by others.

Isaiah Tishby (1908–1993) was born in Hungary and studied at the Hebrew University of Jerusalem, where he wrote his doctoral dissertation on thirteenth-century Kabbala under the supervision of Gershom Scholem. He was Professor of Jewish Mysticism at the Hebrew University and published numerous articles and monographs on the *Zohar*, on the messianic theology of Moshe Hayyim Luzzato and his circle, on Sabbateanism and on Hasidism. Only months before his death, he became the first recipient of the Gershom Scholem Prize for Kabbala Studies, a pentannual award administered by the Israel Academy of Sciences and Humanities.

Ephraim Elimelekh Urbach (1912–1992) was born in Poland and studied in Breslau and Rome, where he earned his doctorate. One of the deans of modern Jewish studies and recipient of the 1955 Israel Prize in that field, he taught rabbinic and talmudic literature at the Hebrew University and published what became standard works on the development of rabbinic Judaism, as well as essays on contemporary issues concerning Judaism and the Jewish people. He served as President of the World Union of Jewish Studies and also as President of the Israel Academy of Sciences and Humanities.

וְהַמַּשְׂכִּלִים יַזְהִרוּ כְּזֹהַר הָרָקִיעַ 'And they that be wise shall shine as the brightness of the firmament...' (Daniel 12:3).

ACKNOWLEDGMENTS

Ziporah Brody deftly translated the six articles in this volume that were originally published in Hebrew, following a symposium held at the Israel Academy of Sciences and Humanities in memory of Gershom Scholem in March 1982. She also edited the article by Joseph Dan. Evelyn Katrak conscientiously proofread the entire volume several times and made many valuable corrections.

Overall editorial responsibility for the volume was assumed by Deborah Greniman of the Publications Department of the Israel Academy of Sciences and Humanities. In addition to editing all the articles for style and accuracy, she supervised the publication of the volume at every stage of production. Her exemplary attention to detail and nuance is itself a tribute to the highest standards of academic excellence set by the man whom this volume honors.

Throughout the various stages of this volume's realization, Hayim Goldgraber offered crucial and ever-gracious assistance.

Nathan Rotenstreich, Vice President of the Israel Academy of Sciences and Humanities, initiated the original memorial meeting from which this volume emerges. Without his unflagging support and dedication to Scholem's legacy, the present English version of the volume would not have come to fruition.

> Jerusalem, July 1993
> Paul Mendes-Flohr

Just hours before this volume was to be sent to the press, we learned of the death of Nathan Rotenstreich (1914–1993). Virtually the last of his generation of scholars who laid the foundations of humanistic culture in Israel, Rotenstreich bore with a commanding erudition and quiet dignity the European intellectual heritage wedded to a firm and knowledgeable commitment to Judaism as a living and ever-renewed spiritual discourse.

We must here record our profound sense of loss of a true friend, colleague and *spiritus rector*.

> Jerusalem, October 1993

CONTENTS

Abbreviations of works by Gershom Scholem   xi

Introductory Essay: The Spiritual Quest of the Philologist
   Paul Mendes-Flohr   1
Gershom Scholem and Judaic Studies
   Ephraim E. Urbach   29
Gershom Scholem's Contribution to the Study of the *Zohar*
   Isaiah Tishby   40
Gershom Scholem on Pantheism in the Kabbala
   J. Ben-Shlomo   56
Gershom Scholem and Jewish Messianism
   Joseph Dan   73
Gershom Scholem's Interpretation of Hasidism as an Expression of
   His Idealism
   Rivka Schatz   87
Gershom Scholem's Conception of Jewish Nationalism
   Nathan Rotenstreich   104
Gershom Scholem as Bibliophile
   Malachi Beit-Arié   120

ABBREVIATIONS OF WORKS
BY GERSHOM SCHOLEM

Devarim be-go = *Devarim be-go — Pirqe morasha ve-tehiya* (Explications and implications — Writings on Jewish heritage and renaissance), Tel Aviv 1975 (in Hebrew)

Herrera = *Avraham Cohen Herrera ve-sefer sha'ar ha-shamayim — Hayyav, yezirato ve-hashpa'ata* (Abraham Cohen Herrera and the book *Sha'ar ha-shamayim* — His life, his work and its influence), Jerusalem 1978 (in Hebrew)

Jewish Gnosticism = *Jewish Gnosticism, Merkabah Mysticism and Talmudic Tradition*, New York 1965

Jews and Judaism = *On Jews and Judaism in Crisis*, New York 1976

Kabbalah and Symbolism = *On the Kabbalah and Its Symbolism*, New York 1965

Kabbalah = *Kabbalah*, Jerusalem 1974. Contains revised versions of many of the articles on Jewish mysticism published in the *Encyclopedia Judaica*, Jerusalem–New York 1972

Major Trends = *Major Trends in Jewish Mysticism*, third revised edition, New York 1961 (first edition Jerusalem 1941)

Messianic Idea = *The Messianic Idea in Judaism and Other Essays on Jewish Spirituality*, New York 1971

Mystical Idea of the Godhead = *On the Mystical Idea of the Godhead*, New York 1976

'Schöpfung' = 'Schöpfung aus Nichts und Selbstverschränkung Gottes,' *Eranos Jahrbuch*, XXV (1956), pp. 87–119

'Ten Unhistorical Aphorisms' = 'Zehn unhistorische Sätze über Kabbalah,' *Judaica*, III — *Studien zur jüdischen Mystik*, Frankfurt a/M 1973; reprinted in D. Biale, 'Gershom Scholem's Ten Unhistorical Aphorisms on Kabbalah: Text and Commentary,' *Modern Judaism*, V (1985), pp. 67–93. The English translations in this volume are based on Biale's commentary.

INTRODUCTORY ESSAY:
THE SPIRITUAL QUEST OF THE PHILOLOGIST

by

Paul Mendes-Flohr[*]

IN JULY 1937, Gershom Scholem received a letter from Stephen Wise inviting him to deliver the following year's Hilda Stroock Lectures at the Jewish Institute of Religion in New York City.[1] Rabbi Wise suggested a series of five or six lectures presenting an overview of the history of Jewish mysticism, a subject Scholem had been teaching at the Hebrew University of Jerusalem since 1925. Scholem accepted with alacrity.[2] He welcomed the opportunity to present, for the first time, the 'principal results'[3] of his labors of more than twenty years in the fledgling discipline he had pioneered, the academic study of Kabbala. He had reached a stage in his research where he felt ready, indeed eager, to depart from detailed philological research and make a synthetic statement. After publishing more than a hundred and fifty scholarly essays laboriously dating texts, identifying authorship, and clarifying terms and concepts,[4] the contours of what he called 'a great and significant chapter' in the history of the Jewish religion had become 'less blurred':

---

[*] Paul Mendes-Flohr is Professor of Modern Jewish Thought and Intellectual History at The Hebrew University of Jerusalem.

[1] Stephen Wise to Gershom Scholem, letter dated 28 June 1937, Gershom Scholem Archives, The Jewish National and University Library, Jerusalem, varia 1599, No. 4.

[2] See Scholem's enthusiastic reply to Wise, dated 16 August 1937, Gershom Scholem Archive (as above, note 1).

[3] *Major Trends*, Preface to the First Edition, p. vii.

[4] For a complete listing of the numerous studies that preceded the Stroock lectures, see the *Bibliography of the Writings of Gershom G. Scholem*, Jerusalem 1967.

1

[Gradually] there emerged from the confusing welter of fact and fiction a picture ... of the development of Jewish mysticism, its inner significance, its problems and its meaning for the history of Judaism in general.[5]

It was no mean task that Scholem had taken upon himself, especially since the lectures would be in English. Hitherto he had written only in German and Hebrew. In a letter of 29 November 1937 to his dear friend Walter Benjamin, he explained his difficulty with a typical touch of irony:

My work at the moment consists of formulating my New York lectures, which I have to deliver in English. That is a very unfamiliar task and costs a lot of time. The art of composing short sentences is not something that attracted my attention in the past.[6]

These lectures served as the basis for Scholem's signal work, *Major Trends in Jewish Mysticism.*[7] It is now just over fifty years since the first publication of that volume, which traces the development of Jewish mystical thought from its beginnings in antiquity to the eighteenth-century movement of Hasidism. Few books of scholarship have enjoyed such impact, fructifying the discourse not only of the academic community but also of the educated public at large. With a rare ability to weave dazzling erudition into lucid, engaging prose, Scholem presented a picture that revolutionized the regnant conception of Judaism, its spiritual interior and its religious

5 *Major Trends, loc. cit.* (above, note 3).
6 Scholem to Benjamin, 29 November 1937, in Gershom Scholem (ed.), *The Correspondence of Walter Benjamin and Gershom Scholem, 1932–1940* (English transl. from the German by Gary Smith and Andre Lefevere), with an introduction by Anson Rabinbach, New York 1989, p. 210.
7 The second and third chapters of *Major Trends*, although prepared for the Stroock Lectures, were delivered not in that series but on other occasions. The volume's title was suggested by Wise in his letter to Scholem cited in note 1 above.

2

consciousness, as well as the role of mysticism in the development of theistic religions in general.

Scholem's Conception of Jewish Mysticism

At the outset of his lectures, Scholem argued forcefully that

> there is no such thing as mysticism in the abstract. ... There is no mysticism as such, there is only the mysticism of a particular religious system, Christian, Islamic, Jewish mysticism and so on.[8]

To be sure, there are shared characteristics that allow for a comparative analysis of various mystical systems, but nonetheless the mystical experience and quest always take place within the context of a particular religious culture, with its distinctive conceptual universe, mode of discourse, texts, traditions, rites and rituals.

One is reminded of a story told by another student of Jewish mysticism, Abraham Joshua Heschel: An elderly gentleman in Berlin used to take a daily stroll in one of that city's public gardens, and there sit on a bench under his favorite tree, resting in the tranquil environs. One day, however, a stranger appeared at the far end of the bench, holding a fiddle and playing it with a relentless fury. Although disturbed by the cacophonous medley, the gentleman said nothing, and despite the vast expanse of the garden, the fiddler returned every day to share the same bench. Scratching away on his ill-tuned instrument, he seemed oblivious to everything around him. The gentleman held his peace, for after all it was a public garden. Perhaps he hoped that the fiddler would eventually move on, but, alas, he didn't. Exasperated, the gentleman finally addressed his musically inept neighbor. With a refinement becoming his station, he gently asked him: 'Excuse me, Sir, which composer are you playing?' 'Oh, no one in particular,' replied the fiddler. 'Just music in general!'[9]

---

8 *Major Trends*, pp. 5f.
9 I am grateful to Harold Schimmel for this story, which he heard at a lecture Heschel delivered at the University of Toronto in the spring of 1954.

The melody or melodies of Jewish mysticism, which Scholem sought to resonate in his scholarship, were specific and distinctive to Judaism. Comparative study and the attendant general statements about the nature of mysticism might, indeed, illuminate some of its features and topoi, but in the end Jewish mysticism could properly be understood only as a 'concrete historical phenomenon.'[10]

The mystic's quest is always bound to a given historical and religious reality, and the Jewish mystic thus seeks to fulfill the desire to 'taste and see' the divine Presence[11] within the context of Judaism: its commandments (*mitzvot*) and liturgy, and its sacred texts, legal and speculative (*halakha* and *aggada*). The mystic assumes that all the varied spiritual impulses informing the life of Jewish piety constitute a sacred reality, and as such are the matrix for the mystical experience. They are a sacramental universe that, properly approached, may serve to quicken the Presence of God.

Scholem highlights the sacramental attitude of Jewish mysticism by comparing its hermeneutics to those of the medieval Jewish philosophers. The mystic, Scholem observes, was wont to view Judaism's concrete manifestations, including the historical fate of the Jews, as *symbols* pointing to hidden, divine truths, while the philosopher preferred to interpret them as *allegories*, reflecting universal truths of reason. The truths of the philosopher, Scholem emphasizes, are not distinctive to religion, that is, to Judaism, but are independently verifiable. Treated as an allegory, the Torah functions as a unique vehicle of philosophic truth:

> The documents of religion are therefore not conceived as expressing a distinct and separate world of religious truth and reality, but rather as giving a simplified description of the relations which exist between the ideas of philosophy. ... In other words, the philosopher can only proceed with his proper task after having successfully converted the concrete realities of Judaism into a bundle of abstractions. The individual phenomenon is to

10 *Major Trends*, p. 6.
11 Scholem cites the verse 'O taste and see that the Lord is good' (Ps. 34:9) and observes, 'it is this tasting and seeing, however spiritualized it may become, that the genuine mystic desires' (*Major Trends*, p. 4).

4

him no object of his philosophical speculation. By contrast, the mystic refrains from destroying the living texture of religious narrative by allegorizing it.[12]

The concept of allegory, Scholem underscores, assumes that sacred language is representational and expressive of some basic facts or truths, and as such is given to translation. Hence, allegory is understood to be the figurative translation or representation of verities that may be expressed by philosophers — and ultimately more clearly and precisely — in an abstract, conceptually refined fashion. In contrast, the appeal to mystical symbols presupposes that a given expression of the Jew's religious reality is an essential aspect of the truth it is meant to disclose; indeed, symbols are intrinsic manifestations of a truth otherwise inexpressible. The mystical symbol is to be likened to an iceberg: its concrete manifestation is palpable and real, but it is only the 'tip' of a greater, hidden reality.[13] So it is with the Torah and all its attendant expressions in the 'living texture' of Jewish religious life. Hence, Scholem underscored, while the philosophers tended to ignore all that was not given to allegorization, the mystics regarded all of Judaism as alive with symbolic significance.

Accordingly, since Jewish religious law resisted allegory, it generally remained alien to philosophical reflection. Even for thinkers like Maimonides who were themselves halakhic scholars, it 'furnished no material for [their] thoughts.'[14] For the mystics, on the other hand, the *halakha* was effervescent with symbolic meaning; it was 'transformed [by them] into a sacrament, a mystery rite. ... Every *mitswah* became an event of cosmic importance, an act which had a bearing upon the dynamics of the universe.'[15] Through the life of Torah and *mitzvot*, the Jews became protagonists in a cosmic drama in which not only the world and Israel are redeemed, but also God Himself.

---

12 *Ibid.*, p. 26.
13 The image of the mystical symbol as an iceberg was employed by the late Alexander Altmann in his lectures on Kabbala, which I attended at Brandeis University in the late 1960s.
14 *Major Trends*, p. 28.
15 *Ibid.*, pp. 30f.

The kabbalists, then, did not hesitate to introduce myth and theurgy into Judaism. For the mystics, Scholem emphasizes, the living God of Israel was, indeed, a *living* being, and they were thus deeply offended by attempts to present Him as a philosophical or theological proposition. Unlike their philosophical colleagues, the mystics were less concerned with securing God's transcendence than with celebrating His immanence, with 'tasting and seeing' His palpable Presence within creation and human experience. The mystics therefore did not flinch from anthropomorphism, the *bête noire* of the philosophers.

Scholem warmly endorsed Franz Rosenzweig's observation that the 'anthropomorphism' of the Kabbala — and that of the rabbinic *aggada* before it — actually provided a 'protective wall ... [safeguarding] monotheism.' Should biblical faith seek to be utterly pure and resist all forms of anthropomorphism, Rosenzweig explained, it would actually open itself up to the threat of polytheism and its unbridled humanization of divinity:

> [For] failing the courage to attribute one's genuinely perceived experiences of God to their genuine and immediate source in God, these experiences [invariably] assume an independent existence and seek for themselves their own supporting entity or entities alongside God Himself whom they had assumed incapable of sustaining them. The farther into the distance God is banished, the more permissible it seems for man to populate with demi-gods and godlings that space between himself and God which is so full of currents of divine energy.[16]

Borne by an 'unshakable certitude that everything we experience of God comes indeed from Him,'[17] the anthropomorphism — and attendant mythic images — of the Kabbala, Rosenzweig noted, affirmed Israel's faith in a living God and subtly fended off the intrusion of pagan myth. Scholem concurred with Rosenzweig's

---

16 F. Rosenzweig, 'A Note on Anthropomorphism' (English transl. by B. Barsky), in F.A. Rothschild (ed.), *Jewish Perspectives on Christianity*, New York 1990, p. 227.
17 *Ibid.*, p. 228.

6

insight that a living faith in the God of Israel requires a touch of anthropomorphism.[18]

Kabbala and Myth

The theistic myth of the Kabbala, according to Scholem, thus not only affirms the living reality of God, but also represents a refined stage of religious consciousness. The most primitive stage, according to Scholem, is indeed the world of pagan myth, in which gods are everywhere; one thus encounters their presence without ecstatic or mystical mediation. In the next stage, in which the monotheistic religions emerge, God is conceived as a transcendent being, thus shattering the 'dream-harmony of Man, Universe and God'[19] and leaving the human being frightfully isolated and alone. This is the classical form of religion, in which the vast gulf between the infinite God and finite humanity cannot be bridged save by the voice of God, through revelation, and by the voice of humanity, in prayer (and obedient submission to God's Word). 'The great monotheistic religions live and unfold in the ever-present consciousness... of [this] abyss' between a God and humanity.[20]

Mysticism marks the next stage of religious consciousness, but far from denying the abyss, it is actually sparked by a particularly acute awareness of the distance that separates humanity and God. Eager to draw closer to God than prayer and obedience to the divine law seem to permit, the mystic seeks a hidden path leading to God. Through a more direct communion with God, the mystic also hopes to restore the unity that was disrupted by the advent of monotheistic faith and its projection of God to a transcendent, supernal abode. So myth, primed by the quest to revalorize the harmonious unity between all of creation and the Divine Reality, is born anew within Judaism. But the

---

18 Scholem voiced his approval for Rosenzweig's views on the anthropomorphic tension inherent in biblical faiths in response to a paper on the subject by Moshe Idel, presented at a conference held in May 1980 in Jerusalem to mark the fiftieth anniversary of Rosenzweig's death. See M. Idel, 'Franz Rosenzweig and the Kabbala,' in P. Mendes-Flohr (ed.), *The Philosophy of Franz Rosenzweig*, Hanover, N.H., 1988, pp. 162–171.

19 *Major Trends*, p. 7.

20 *Ibid.*

myth of the mystics, Scholem stresses, is hardly a naive withdrawal
to the monistic universe of the pre-theistic mythological sensibility.
In Hegelian terms, there is a sublation (*Aufhebung*), a dialectical
reconciliation between theistic faith and the intense awareness of
God's Presence characteristic of mythic consciousness. As Scholem
succinctly puts it, in mysticism 'the world of mythology and that of
revelation meet in the soul of man.'[21] The resulting theistic myth —
so rife with paradox — generates tensions and theologoumena that
preoccupy Jewish mysticism.

Kabbala and Pantheism

Hence, while attesting to the primordial unity of all existence, a fact
grounded in the Unity of God Himself, the mystic is also painfully
aware — scandalized, one might say — by the abiding contradictions
of quotidian experience, especially the reality of evil and inexplicable
suffering that blights human existence. The mystic accepts no easy
answers exculpating God. The traditional theodicies will not do.
Struggling with the question of evil, even as articulated by the
heretical Gnostics, the mystic recognizes evil as a brute, perhaps
autonomous reality, while never relinquishing a fervent affirmation
of the world as Creation, as a divine blessing. The paradox, Scholem
notes, did not bother the mystics; on the contrary, it only fired their
rich imagination. It was deepened by the mystics' pull to pantheism,
their eager desire to discern the hidden life of God in all of creation.
As Joseph Ben-Shlomo indicates in this volume, Scholem showed
how most Jewish mystics delicately maintained the fine line between
pantheism and a theistic conception of God's transcendence.

The overarching solution the kabbalists found to this vexing
paradox is characterized by Scholem as panentheism: the world is
manifestly within God, but not identical with Him. By thus affirming
God's abiding transcendence, the Kabbala preserved the monotheistic conception of history. In contrast to pagan and pantheistic myth,
which, lacking a concept of a transcendent God, did not pose a divine
scheme of history (*Heilsgeschichte*), Jewish mysticism continued to
regard history as the arena in which humanity's relationship to God

21 *Ibid.*, p. 8.

8

is fully realized, and in which redemption takes place. The tensions unique to kabbalistic doctrines of redemption, as understood by Scholem, are discussed in Joseph Dan's contribution to the volume.

Kabbala and Hasidism

Within the history of both Kabbala and messianism, the phenomenon of Hasidism — the popular mystical movement that arose in the eighteenth century and transformed the spiritual physiognomy of much of Eastern European Jewry — is often regarded as *sui generis*. Not only did the movement popularize esoteric teachings that had hitherto been entrusted to a spiritual elite, but it effectively counteracted trends toward messianic activism. The popularization of the often recondite kabbalistic doctrines was achieved, according to Scholem, by conflating mystical and ethical values, thus rendering Kabbala a personal creed accessible to the simplest of Jews; Hasidism, in the pithy characterization of Martin Buber, was 'Kabbala become ethos' ('Ethos gewordenen Kabbala'), a formulation Scholem approvingly cited.[22] With respect to messianism, Hasidism 'neutralized'[23] intense apocalyptic expectations of an imminent advent of the Redeemer — such as those that swept parts of the Jewish world with the seventeenth-century Sabbatean movement — by placing the *zaddiq* or *rebbe* at the center of its spiritual life. Generally a charismatic personality who served as a mystical teacher and soteriological agent, the *zaddiq* aided his followers or Hasidim in attaining a degree of spiritual (as opposed to historical) salvation in the here and now. Scholem sought to explain the unique position of Hasidism in Jewish spiritual history, as Rivka Schatz explains in this volume, by exploring the phenomenological significance of the new form of religious leadership represented by the *zaddiq*. Schatz also shows how Scholem's approach to the study of Hasidism was determined by his ambivalent evaluation of Buber's interpretation of the movement.

---

22 Cf. M. Buber, *The Tales of Rabbi Nachman* (English transl. from the German by Maurice Friedman), with an introduction by P. Mendes-Flohr and Z. Gries, Atlantic Highlands, N.J., 1988, p. 10; cited without source reference by Scholem in *Major Trends*, p. 342.

23 *Major Trends*, p. 329.

Paul Mendes-Flohr

Kabbalistic Hermeneutics

The remarkable ability of Hasidism — as of Kabbala in general —
to introduce bold innovations in Jewish doctrine (and practice) while
remaining within the pale of tradition was, Scholem avers, due prin-
cipally to its hermeneutics, its reverential but daring interpretation
of the sacred texts informing the cognitive and normative horizons
of the tradition. Unlocking new, hidden meanings in those texts,
the kabbalists allowed the tradition to unfold as a dynamic process,
accommodating new impulses and responding to new historical
and cultural realities confronting the Jew; in their hands, Jewish
tradition became a dialectical interplay of normative and novel, even
heterodox ideas. Significantly, Scholem pointed out, the very term
Kabbala means tradition, or literally 'that which is received' — a
secret, hence somehow deeper knowledge of God's Word, received
from the past. The Kabbala does not present itself as an alternative
tradition, but rather as offering insight into the more profound levels
of meaning embedded in the teachings that have guided Israel since
Sinai. It is a general characteristic of mysticism as a phenomenon of
historical religions, Scholem argues, to regard itself as conforming
with tradition:

> It lies in the very nature of mysticism as a specific phenomenon
> within historical systems of religion that two conflicting tenden-
> cies should converge in it. Since historical mysticism does not
> hover in space, but is a mystical view of a specific reality; since it
> subjects the positive contents of a concrete phenomenon such as
> Judaism, Christianity, or Islam to a new, mystical interpretation
> without wishing to come into conflict with the living reality
> and traditions of these religions, mystical movements face a
> characteristic contradiction. On the one hand, the new view of
> God and often enough of the world cloaks itself in the deli-
> berately conservative attitude of men who are far from wishing
> to infringe on, let alone, overthrow tradition, but wish rather to
> strengthen it with the help of their new vision. Yet, on the other
> hand, despite this attitude of piety toward tradition, the element
> of novelty in the impulses that are here at work is often enough

10

reflected in a bold, if not sacrilegious, transformation of the traditional religious contents. This tension between conservative and innovationist or even revolutionary tendencies runs through the whole history of mysticism.[24]

From this perspective, as Scholem often emphasized, Kabbala serves to remind us that there is no 'essence' of Judaism, no normative, fast definition:

[It] cannot be defined according to its essence, since it has no essence. Judaism cannot therefore be regarded as a closed historical phenomenon whose development and essence came into focus by a finite sequence of historical, philosophical, doctrinal, or dogmatic judgments and statements.[25]

Primed by an ongoing rereading and thus subtle reformulation of the tradition, Judaism is rather a 'living entity,' whose 'systematic truth' is to be comprehended only in the 'totality' of its historical manifestations.[26]

Because of their insistent efforts to weave their experience and vision into the tradition and especially into its sacred texts, Scholem held, Jewish mystics rarely found their voice in personal mystical

---

24 'Tradition and New Creation in the Ritual of the Kabbalists,' in *Kabbala and Symbolism*, p. 118.

25 G. Scholem, 'Judaism,' in A.A. Cohen and P. Mendes-Flohr (eds.), *Contemporary Jewish Religious Thought: Original Essays on Critical Concepts, Movements, and Beliefs*, New York 1987, p. 505.

26 See Scholem's October 1937 birthday greeting to the publisher Salman Schocken, in D. Biale, *Gershom Scholem: Kabbalah and Counter-History*, Cambridge 1979, pp. 76 (English) and 216 (German). Scholem's non-essentialist view of Judaism parallels that of the German Christian historian Ernst Troeltsch (1865–1923). Opposing Adolf von Harnack's argument in his exceedingly popular volume *What is Christianity?* (1900), Troeltsch declared that Christianity can only be understood in its 'totality'; Christianity *is* its history. Thus the essence of Christianity can be understood only as the productive power of the historical Christian religion to create new interpretations and new adaptations — a power that lies deeper than any historical formulation which it may have produced. Cf. E. Troeltsch, 'The Dogmatics of the Religionsgeschichtliche Schule,' *American Journal of Theology* (January 1913), pp. 12–13.

11

testimony or ecstatic confessions.[27] They tended rather to articulate their experience through a highly creative hermeneutical fantasy, frequently directed to theosophical speculations probing the inner life of the Godhead palpitating just below the surface of the texts, indeed the entire texture of existence. The Kabbala thus 'comes to the rescue of tradition,'[28] freeing it from the dangers of spiritual stagnation and desiccation. Re-interpreting the sacred texts, the mystics revalorize Jewish tradition, endowing it with a new vitality, an intellectually and existentially engaging content.

Scholem and Buber's Erlebnis-*Mysticism*

The primacy that the kabbalists gave to the hermeneutic moment over the mystical experience *per se*, in Scholem's judgment, was the source of its creative power *within* Judaism.[29] This view corresponds to his own personal position that for any religious experience to have cultural resonance, it must be grounded in a tradition and its sacred texts. Specifically, the contemporary renewal of Judaism must begin with the retrieval by its deracinated sons and daughters of Jewish textual literacy — a conviction that crystallized already in Scholem's youth. Emerging from the assimilation of his parental home, his initial steps toward Judaism and a Zionist commitment to the renewal of a Jewish national identity and culture drew him, like so many of his generation of young Jews, to the teachings of Martin Buber. In this period, Buber addressed central-European Jewish youth estranged from what they perceived as the moribund traditions of Judaism. He taught that the tradition need not be an impediment to a meaningful relationship to Judaism, for it could be circumvented

27 As Scholem says on p. 15 of *Major Trends*, 'The Kabbalists ... are no friends of mystical autobiography.'
28 *Major Trends*, p. 23.
29 *Ibid.*, p. 23: 'The secret of the success of the Kabbalah lies in the nature of its relation to the spiritual heritage of rabbinical Judaism. This relation differs from that of rationalist philosophy, in that it is more deeply and in a more vital sense connected with the main forces in Judaism.' Kabbalah remains attuned to these forces — viz., the *halakha*, *aggada*, and liturgy — by the art of rereading the sacred texts such that they now reflect new insights, values and meaning.

12

by tapping Judaism's core primal experience (*Urerlebnis*), which he vaguely but alluringly described as an intense emotional experience (*Erlebnis*) — as opposed to a purely conceptual understanding — of the fundamental unity of life, despite one's ordinary, sensate experience (*Erfahrung*) of its fragmented, divisive character.[30] One had only to live in accord with this *Urerlebnis*, seeking a consistency between one's inner affective life and one's outer deeds. Stated with the inflections of the then fashionable Expressionism, Buber's message fascinated the young Scholem, as it did countless others. But as Rivka Schatz notes, Scholem soon grew wary of Buber's teaching; suspicious of what he regarded as its self-consciously aestheticized, affected manner, he sensed a nigh-total lack of real content.

Scholem's friendship with Walter Benjamin was sealed by his discovery of their mutual disaffection with Buber's *Erlebnis*-mysticism. In an entry in his diary, Scholem records his impressions of his first meeting with Benjamin, which quickly led to their lasting friendship. They met in August 1916 through mutual acquaintances at the Bavarian resort of Seeshaupt, and over a period of several days the nineteen-year-old Scholem and the twenty-four-year-old Benjamin engaged in a marathon discussion about matters of mutual concern:

> During our entire period together we spoke an awfully lot about Judaism: about going to Palestine and 'agrarian Zionism,' about Ahad Ha-Am and 'justice,' but mostly about Buber, from whom after these four days not so much as anything remained. Benjamin was not wrong, when as he bade me farewell he said, were I to meet Buber I should give him in our name a barrel of tears (*Tränenfass*). Not that I learned anything in this matter from Benjamin. On the contrary, for more than nine months I thought exactly the same as he; only one point now became also

---

30 See M. Buber, *Drei Reden über das Judentum*, Frankfurt a/M 1911, and 'Addresses on Judaism,' in idem, *On Judaism*, ed. N.N. Glatzer (English transl. by E. Jospe), New York 1967, pp. 11–55. Cf. G. Scholem, 'Buber's Conception of Judaism,' in *Jews and Judaism*, pp. 126–171; and see also P. Mendes-Flohr, *From Mysticism to Dialogue: Martin Buber and the Transformation of German Social Thought*, Detroit 1989, pp. 49–82.

verbally clear to me: the repudiation of the value of *Erlebnis*.
From here is the question, the 'key-question,' one may say:
'Have you already had the Jewish *Erlebnis?*' ('Haben Sie schon
das jüdische Erlebnis gehabt?') ... Benjamin sought to induce
me to include in [an article I was to write on Buber and his
youthful followers],[31] a decisive rejection of *Erlebnis*-cronies:
Down with *Erlebnis!*[32]

Benjamin and Scholem concluded that an immediate experience
of God, independent of tradition, is ultimately elusive. For Jews
such as themselves, products of the purgatory of assimilation and
secularization, the divine reality could only be experienced via the
mediation of traditional texts, bearing as they do the traces of a
numinous reality informing them. One thus reads those texts with
the hope of revalorizing that reality for oneself.

Overcoming History by History

But the texts are now encrusted by the relativizing sneer of modern
historical scholarship, which denies the events and creations of
bygone ages privileged access to absolute values and truth. How
then, Scholem asked himself, is a person burdened by the modern
historicist bias to gain entry to the past and the truths to which it
laid claim? The young Scholem set out upon the path of historical
reconstruction, employing the most rigorous tools of the philologist
to peel away the debris of time and recapture the voices hidden in the
texts he studied. Here he assumed a task he regarded as inherently
ironic — using the historian's tools to overcome history and the
curse of relativism.[33] In the first of his 'Ten Unhistorical Aphorisms
on Kabbala,' written in 1958, he pondered whether the 'philologist'
— as he preferred to call himself because of his exacting attention

31 Cf. G. Scholem, 'Jüdische Jugendbewegung,' *Der Jude*, I (1916–1917), pp.
822–825.
32 Idem, unpublished diaries, entry dated 23–24 August 1916, cited in G.
Smith, *Benjaminiana*, Giessen 1991, pp. 56–59.
33 Again, as suggested in note 26 above, Scholem may be compared to
Troeltsch, who spoke of 'overcoming history by history.' See note 65
below.

14

to linguistic and conceptual detail — did not compound 'the mist' that shrouds the past:

> Does there remain for the philologist something visible in this mist ... or does the essential [aspect of that which is studied] disappear in this projection of the historical? The uncertainty in answering this question is inherent in the nature of the philological enterprise itself and thus the hope, from which this works draws its life, retains something ironic which cannot be severed from it. ... But is not such irony that much more when it resides already in the subject matter itself, Kabbala, and not only in its history?[34]

For the Kabbala speaks of hidden truths, which at most can be but inadequately transmitted. How, then, can the historian ever hope to behold these truths? For the historian as for the kabbalist, *mutatis mutandis*, 'authentic tradition remains hidden; only the decaying tradition (*verfallende Tradition*) falls upon (*verfällt auf*) a subject and only in its fallen state (*im Verfall*) does its greatness become visible.'[35]

---

34 'Ten Unhistorical Aphorisms,' pp. 70–71.
35 *Ibid.*, p. 71. In his commentary on Scholem's aphorisms, David Biale judiciously points out that the analogy between the historian and the kabbalist must be understood metaphorically:

> The problem of the historian differs fundamentally from that of the Kabbalist. Although both confront truths which are inaccessible to ordinary sense perception, the secrecy of Kabbalistic truth is a result of the *transcendence* of God, while the historian deals with events which are part of the world. Historical truth is only 'secret' in the sense that what lies beyond the temporal horizon of the historian is unknowable in the perceptual sense of the word, while Kabbalistic knowledge is secret because God is essentially absent. Thus, only by metaphorically conceiving of the past as somehow parallel to the hiddennes of God does the analogy between the historian and the Kabbalist make sense (*ibid.*, p. 72).

The analogy, however, can be taken more literally if we assume, as indeed seems to have been the case, that Scholem understood his own ultimate objective as an historian of Kabbala as being not only to recover the meaning of the texts he investigated but also to retrieve the divine truths or reality that inspired those texts.

Kafka as a Secularized Kabbalist

Here is where the kabbalist and the modern historian meet: both, in Scholem's view, are heirs to a fallen — decayed, corrupted — tradition. In his 'unhistorical' aphorisms, Scholem removes the professorial robes of the historian and speaks in a quasi-autobiographical voice, bearing witness to his personal, existential agenda as a student of Jewish mysticism. In the tenth and last aphorism, he elliptically alludes to his affinity to Franz Kafka, noting that the writings of the Czech-Jewish author are in effect a 'secularized presentation of a kabbalistic world-feeling.'[36] Significantly, he traces Kafka's spiritual lineage back to the Prague Frankist Jonas Wehle (1752–1823). As Scholem admiringly remarks, this exponent of a heretical Kabbala and nihilistic messianism, speaking in the language of the Enlightenment, was 'the first to pose the question (answering in the affirmative) whether with the banishment of humankind from its midst Paradise had not lost more than humankind itself.'[37] Kafka implicitly asks a similar question, and this, Scholem suggests, is no mere coincidence: 'Perhaps because we do not know what has happened with Paradise, Kafka ... regarded any consideration of "why the good" to be "in a certain sense hopeless".'[38] Another reference to Kafka appears in Scholem's 1937 birthday greeting to Salman Schocken, disarmingly entitled 'A Candid Word about the True Motives of My Kabbalistic Studies':

> Many exciting thoughts had led me [in the years 1916–1918] ... to an intuitive affirmation of mystical propositions [*Thesen*] which walked the fine line between religion and nihilism. I later [found in Kafka] the most perfect and unsurpassed expression of this fine line, an expression which, as a secular statement of the kabbalistic world-feeling in a modern spirit, seemed to me to wrap Kafka's writings in the halo of the canonical.[39]

36 'Ten Unhistorical Aphorisms,' p. 88 (translation is mine).
37 *Ibid.*
38 *Ibid.*
39 Cited in D. Biale, *Kabbalah and Counter-History* (above, note 26), p. 75 (I have slightly emended Biale's translation).

For Scholem, Kafka was emblematic of the modern Jew whose feeling is of clinging skeptically, yet reverentially, to the thin strands of a frayed tradition. It was this ambivalence of a secularized Jew with an abiding religious sensiblity that lay behind Scholem's definition of himself as a 'religious anarchist.'[40] As Rivka Schatz illuminates, Scholem's brand of religious anarchism was different in kind from Buber's, of which he was highly critical. He was an anarchist not out of abstract principle but because of his metaphysical uncertainty, and his consequent existential anguish regarding the source of religious authority.[41] He therefore saw in Kafka a kindred soul, as he explained in a detailed epistolatory exchange with Benjamin. Along with one of his letters, he sent Benjamin a copy of Kafka's *The Trial*, enclosing with it, on a separate sheet, a poem in which he recorded his vision of Kafka in epigrammatic verse:

Are we totally separated from you?
Is there not a breath of your peace,
Lord, or your message
Intended for us in such a night?

Can the sound of your word
Have so faded in Zion's emptiness,
Or had it not even entered
This magic realm of appearance?

The great deceit of the world
Is now consummated.

40 See 'Dialectic of Continuity and Rebellion' (an interview with Scholem), in E. Ben-Ezer (ed.), *Unease in Zion*, New York 1974, pp. 279f.
41 Cf. Scholem's statement at a July 1939 meeting of a Jerusalem study circle, *Ha'ol*:
   Our anarchism is transitional. ... We are the living example that this [anarchism] does not remove one from Judaism. We are a generation not without commandments (*mitzvot*), but our commandments are bereft of authority. But I don't have an inferiority complex *vis-à-vis* the Orthodox. We are no less legimate than our forefathers, they simply had a clearer text. We are perhaps anarchists, but we are opposed to anarchy.
   For the full citation and a commentary, see P. Mendes-Flohr, *Divided Passions: Jewish Intellectuals and the Experience of Modernity*, Detroit 1991, pp. 400f.

Give then, Lord, that he may wake
Who was struck through by your nothingness.

Only so does revelation
Shine in the time that rejected you.
Only your nothingness is the experience [*Erfahrung*]
It is entitled to have of you.

Thus alone teaching that breaks through semblance
Enters the memory:
The truest bequest
Of hidden judgment.

Our position has been measured
On Job's scales with great precision.
We are known through and through
As despairing as on the youngest day.

What we are is reflected
In endless instances.
Nobody knows the way completely
And each part of it makes us blind.

No one can benefit from redemption.
That star stands far too high.
And if you had arrived there too,
You would still stand in your way.

Abandoned to powers,
Exorcism is no longer binding.
No life can unfold
That doesn't sink into itself.

From the center of destruction
A ray breaks though at times,
But none shows the direction
The Law ordered us to take.

Since this sad knowledge
Stands before us, unassailable,
A veil has suddenly been torn,
Lord, before your majesty.

Your trial began on earth.
Does it end before your throne?
You cannot be defended,
As no illusion holds true here.

Who is the accused here?
The creature or yourself?
If anyone should ask you,
You would sink into silence.

Can such a question be raised?
Is the answer indefinite?
Oh, we must nonetheless live
Until your court examines us.[42]

In a subsequent letter to Benjamin, Scholem offers his own commentary on the poem: 'Kafka's world is the world of revelation, but a revelation seen of course from that perspective in which it is returned to its own nothingness.'[43] Scholem goes on to explain that it is our very inability to fulfill the Law, which by virtue of our secular sensibility is refracted back into its supernal nothingness (in mystical parlance, the primordial abode of God), that 'offers the key to Kafka's work.'[44] Kafka's problem — and Scholem's — is 'the fact that it [the Law] can not be *fulfilled*.'[45] Shrouded in nothingness, the revealed Word of God cannot be deciphered.[46]

In his perceptive commentary to Scholem's 'Ten Unhistorical Aphorisms,' David Biale observes that

> the notion of the hiddenness of the source of revelation was surely kabbalistic, but where the Kabbalists claimed to be able

42 Letter of 9 July 1934, in *The Correspondence of Walter Benjamin and Gershom Scholem* (above, note 7), pp. 123–125 (I have somewhat revised the translation).
43 Letter of 17 July 1934, *ibid.*, p. 126.
44 *Ibid.*
45 *Ibid.*
46 For a comprehensive discussion of Scholem's reading of Kafka, see Stéphane Moses, 'Zur Frage des Gesetzes: Gershom Scholems Kafka-Bild,' in K.E. Grözinger, S. Moses, and H.D. Zimmermann (eds.), *Franz Kafka und das Judentum*, Frankfurt a/M 1987, pp. 13–34.

to penetrate these secrets, the secular Jew [as represented by Kafka] remained impotently paralyzed outside the first gate of the Law.[47]

Sharing this sensibility, Scholem went one — or several — steps beyond Kafka. He became a committed Zionist and a historian.

Scholem and the Historian's Task

Inspired by a powerful intuition that Kabbala held within it 'the secret life of Judaism' — where the soul of the Jew struggles with the most exigent questions of faith and perhaps achieves an understanding, however fragmentary, of God's Word — Scholem resolved to write 'not the history but the metaphysics of the Kabbala.'[48] To achieve that goal, he realized that he would first have to penetrate 'the misty wall of history' that beclouds our view of the Kabbala.[49] This decision, as we have already noted, was not free of ambiguity, and it left him pondering, 'Will I get stuck in the mist, will I, so to speak, suffer a "professorial death"?'[50] Nevertheless, the youthful Scholem concluded that 'the necessity of historical criticism and critical history cannot be replaced by anything else.'[51] It is only through 'the singular mirror of philological criticism' that one has 'the hope of a true communication from the mountain.'

Scholem set upon the task he assigned himself with a breathless earnestness. He faced a legacy of neglect fostered by the contemptuous attitudes of nineteenth-century Jewish scholarship toward all that did not conform to a rationalist conception of Judaism. As Scholem was quick to acknowledge, the founding generations of modern Judaic Studies, marching under the banner of what they somewhat bombastically called the Science of Judaism (*Wissenschaft des Judentums*), had made impressive strides in presenting an academically credible accounting of Judaism, particularly its rich religious and

47 'Ten Unhistorical Aphorisms,' pp. 88f.
48 Scholem to Schocken, letter of October 1937, cited in Biale, *Kabbalah and Counter-History* (above, note 26), p. 75.
49 *Ibid.*
50 *Ibid.*, p. 76.
51 *Ibid.*

20

philosophical life. They were guided, however, by an apologetic agenda designed to deflect negative views of Judaism, at a time when Jews increasingly sought acceptance in the evolving liberally bent political and cultural orders of the modern West. Conspicuously absent from the purview of the Science of Judaism was Jewish mysticism, together with other expressions of Judaism that might tarnish the cultural and intellectual 'respectability' Jews then sought to project. The ramified library of Jewish mystical and kabbalistic texts, deemed incompatible with the rational liberal ethos, was studiously ignored, concealed through neglect or summarily dismissed by derisive comments portraying Kabbalism as extraneous to the true spirit of Judaism.

Scholem's attitudes toward the work of his predecessors, and the new directions he sought to introduce into the field of Judaic Studies, are sensitively and incisively described by Ephraim E. Urbach in his essay in this volume. As Scholem noted in the preface to the first edition of *Major Trends*:

> The task which confronted me necessitated a vast amount of spade-work in a field strewn with ruins and by no means ripe as yet for the constructive labors of a builder of a system [allowing for synoptic and metaphysical observations regarding Kabbala]. Both as to historical fact and philological analysis there was pioneer work to be done, often of the most primitive and elementary kind. ... I found myself constrained by inclination to perform the modest but necessary task of clearing the ground of much scattered debris.

Scholem had to rehabilitate singlehandedly not only the image of Kabbala but also its literature, much of it scattered and inaccessible to the scholarly community. With prodigious energy, he assembled the relevant texts, subjected them to meticulous philological analysis, and prepared critical editions. Scholem's awesome devotion to the labors of a philologist is deferentially described in Isaiah Tishby's essay on 'Scholem's Contribution to the Study of the Zohar.'

Scholem was fond of quoting an aphorism coined by the art historian Aby Warburg, 'the dear God lives in details' (*der liebe*

Gott lebt im Detail).[52] These sentiments rang true to him, for he was, according to his own testimony, a philologist by both metaphysical duty and personal disposition. These same inclinations spurred the bibliophilic fervor affectionately depicted in this volume by Malachi Beit-Arié. From early adulthood, he was an indefatigable collector of kabbalistic works, particularly those long lost, out of print, available only in limited editions, or still only in manuscript.

An intellectually and emotionally intense individual, Scholem never allowed his passions to intermingle, keeping his role as a philologist strictly apart from his existential, religious concerns. Towards the end of his life he had occasion to state this position programmatically, in an address entitled 'Identification and Distance' given at the concluding session of the August 1979 Eranos conference. He began with a retrospective appreciation of the thirty years in which he had participated in the annual gatherings. Held in the bucolic Swiss fishing village of Ascona on the shores of Lago Maggiore, the Eranos conferences brought together scholars of the human and natural sciences — comparative religionists, psychologists, philosophers, physicists, and biologists — to deliberate on religious, philosophical and psychological questions. Here Scholem mildly rebuked Olga Froebe, the founder and *spiritus rector* of the conferences, for insisting that the speakers 'identify with their subject matter'[53] in order to ensure spiritual engagement, or what she called *Ergriffenheit* — being seized emotionally by the subject. 'Sie wollte ergriffene Redner, keine Professoren, obwohl sie alle Professoren hiessen' ('she wanted enspirited speakers, no professors, although they were all called professors').[54] Scholem respectfully objected:

> I am actually of the opinion that whosoever identifies fully with his subject loses a certain scholarly measure without which there can be no research. A scholar is not a priest; and it is a mistake to attempt to make a priest out of a scholar.[55]

[52] Scholem, 'The Science of Judaism — Then and Now,' in *Messianic Idea*, p. 313.
[53] G. Scholem, 'Identifizierung und Distanz: Ein Rueckblick,' *Eranos 48 — 1979*, Frankfurt a/M 1981, p. 466.
[54] *Ibid.*
[55] *Ibid.*

'Distance' — scholarly detachment — he explained, 'makes scientific knowledge possible.'[56] The rigid boundaries he sought to maintain between scholarship and personal involvement were dictated by methodological considerations. An objective, emotionally detached posture is necessary in order to attain a full, unbiased picture of a given phenomenon and to detect nuances and processes that might otherwise remain obscured by the rubble of history. But Scholem was no cold historical positivist, content with unearthing and dusting off 'facts' retrieved from the past. Indeed, as both Ephraim E. Urbach and Nathan Rotenstreich show in their respective contributions to this volume, Scholem employed a refined phenomenological method in his reconstruction of the data of the past and their meaning-structures.

Zionism and the Revision of Wissenschaft des Judentums

In response to an article that discerned a theological motive to his scholarship, Scholem vigorously objected, and scribbled in the margins: 'I did not write as a theologian.'[57] And yet, as we have seen, Scholem had theological concerns and a metaphysical agenda, and if they did not intrude upon his scholarship, they surely placed his academic labors in an inner tension with broader, 'extramural' intellectual and spiritual issues that preoccupied him.[58]

He apparently conceived of the relationship between scholarship and theology as a dialectical one, as indicated by the strategic significance he assigned Judaic Studies within Zionism. As sponsored by the movement of Jewish national pride and self-respect, the academic study of Judaism would be utterly free of all apologetic

56 *Ibid.*
57 This comment was written in the margins of a draft of a review by Hyam Maccoby of David Biale's *Kabbalah and Counter-History*. See David N. Myers, *'From Zion Will Go Forth Torah': Jewish Scholarship and the Zionist Return to History* (Ph.D. disseration, Columbia University, 1991), p. 451, n. 117.
58 In his aforementioned Eranos lecture, Scholem admits to such a tension in his work: '... denn viele von uns — ich muss mich selber dazu zählen — sprachen gerade aus der Spannung zwischen diesen beiden Polen,' 'Identifizierung und Distanz' (above, note 53) p. 466.

motives and would achieve a maximum of objectivity. Moreover, viewing Judaism 'as a living organism and not merely as an idea,'[59] Zionism would encourage a vital shift of scholarly horizons. All manifestations of Judaism — even 'the question of the Jewish underworld of the eighteenth and nineteenth centuries: thieves, robbers, and the like'[60] — would be open for review. Of specific importance for Scholem, dispensing with the trammels of apologetics would open to the scrutiny of the scholar all the wellsprings of Jewish tradition, even those disdained as heretical and heterodox by the contemporary custodians of the tradition. In the healing climes of Zion, our very conception of normative Judaism will be radically revised:

> Forces whose value was once denigrated will appear in a different light. Forces which were not considered important enough for serious scholars to research will now be raised from the depths of concealment. Perhaps what was once called degeneracy will now be regarded as a revelation, and what seemed to them [the apologetic scholars of the nineteenth century] to be an impotent hallucination will be revealed as a great and vibrant myth.[61]

Through a truly untendentious Jewish scholarship, Scholem sought to challenge the regnant conception of Jewish tradition upheld by the Orthodox establishment and rejected by those disaffected with it. By tapping forgotten or repressed strata of the Jewish past, Jewish studies would display the multifarious forces of Judaism, and the many faces of tradition. The emerging countenance of Judaism, Scholem was confident, would be more subtle, its lineaments more varied and nuanced than hitherto assumed. Beheld in its fullness, the tradition still had the power to nourish the spiritual and cultural renewal that increasing numbers of modern Jews desired. 'Innova-

59 'The Science of Judaism — Then and Now' (above, note 52), p. 309.
60 *Ibid.*
61 'Mi-tokh hirhurim 'al hokhmat yisra'el,' *Devarim be-go*, p. 399; cited and translated in Myers, 'From Zion' (above, note 57), p. 323.

tion,' Scholem insisted, 'arises not from denying one's tradition,' but from a dialectical affirmation, or 'metamorphosis of tradition.'[62]

Although scholarship was to be pursued according to the strictest canons of objective, scientific inquiry, it was no mere archival ordering of artifacts of the past.[63] On the contrary: the academic study of Judaism, as Scholem envisioned it, was a propaedeutic for Jewish renewal, a preparatory exercise indispensable for the genuine efflorescence of Judaism as a vital, living culture. By re-opening the tradition, Jewish studies would serve to release the hidden wellsprings of Judaism, encouraging them to fecundate the creative energies of contemporary Jews eager to give their inner life a Jewish expression.[64] As Nathan Rotenstreich highlights in his essay on Scholem's national thought, Scholem deemed scholarship a necessary feature of Zionism as a movement sponsoring the spiritual

---

62 G. Scholem, 'Zionism — Dialectic of Continuity and Rebellion' (above, note 40), p. 275.

63 'The Science of Judaism — Then and Now,' p. 308.

64 Again, as suggested in note 26, above, one is struck by the parallels between Scholem's project and that of the German Protestant historian Ernst Troeltsch. In his widely discussed last published work, *Der Historismus and seine Probleme* (1922), Troeltsch endeavored to show how 'history could be overcome by history' (*Gesammelte Schriften*, Berlin 1925, III, p. 772). One's cultural heritage, Troeltsch held, is a storehouse of values, or as Schleiermacher once put it, the plethora of values evolved in a particular culture are 'entrusted to history for safekeeping' (F. Schleiermacher, *The Christian Faith* [English transl. by H. R. Mackintosh and J.S. Stewart], Edinburgh 1928, p. 475). Troeltsch observed that an individual or group faced with making a historical decision has the choice of incorporating in that decision particular values preserved by history, that is, historical memory (which the historian has a decisive role in cultivating). Such decisions, anchored in the values of the past, enjoy cultural continuity while being free, and are thus creatively vital to present need. By virtue of such a perspective, Troeltsch also hoped to avoid both the antiquarian bias of historicism and what Dilthey called the 'anarchy of convictions,' that is, the deadening relativism wrought by the modern historical consciousness. The affinity of such thoughts to Scholem's views becomes that much more patent when Troeltch speaks of the role of historical scholarship in refining the 'historical sense' of a generation, and characterizes the consequent reclaiming of given values of the past to which that historical sense may lead as a 'renaissance' or 'reformation.'

renaissance of a Jewry battered by the forces of assimilation and secularization.[65]

The Origins of This Volume

This volume is based on papers read at a memorial meeting held, in accordance with Jewish custom, thirty days after Scholem's death on 20 February 1982. The meeting was convened at the Israel Academy of Sciences and Humanities, of which Scholem was a founding member, and which he served as president from 1968 to 1974. The papers were given by six of his students and closest colleagues: Malachi Beit-Arié, Joseph Ben-Shlomo, Nathan Rotenstreich, Rivka Schatz, Isaiah Tishby and Ephraim E. Urbach. A seventh essay was later added by Joseph Dan, the first incumbent of the Gershom Scholem Chair in Jewish Mysticism at The Hebrew University, established in tribute to a scholar singularly identified with the founding of that institution and the determination of the image of scholarly excellence that still inspires it.

These scholars represent the first generations of Scholem's students and colleagues at The Hebrew University (except for Malachi Beit-Arié, who had a very close relationship with Scholem in his latter years). Since Scholem's death, a younger generation of scholars of Jewish mysticism has established itself with a rare exuberance and sedulousness in Jerusalem and other centers of learning, in the State of Israel and elsewhere. Indeed, as if in homage to Scholem's memory, there has been a burgeoning of Kabbala studies. The sheer number of scholars now working in the field, at the most prestigious institutions of higher learning in the world, underscores the honored position that the discipline Scholem pioneered has earned in the curriculum of academia.

---

65 On a number of occasions, Scholem registered his bitter disappointment that Zionist tutelage failed to inspire the type of radical revision of Judaic Studies that he had envisioned: 'We came to revolt, and ended up continuing' ('Mi-tokh hirhurim' [above, note 61], p. 402). Scholem's misgivings about the direction Judaic Studies took in Palestine, and later the State of Israel, are discussed by E.E. Urbach in his essay in this volume.

Although manifestly inspired by Scholem's rigorous philological and scholarly standards — not to speak of his awe-inspiring intellectual vistas — the present generation of scholars has not been cowed by its reverence for his magisterial achievement, and has allowed itself to question some of his observations and conclusions, and even his basic premises. Scholem would undoubtedly have been pleased by the independent spirit, openness to new questions, imaginative flair and methodological sophistication they often display in their research. In fact, Scholem, who was disappointed that his contemporaries did not free their research from extraneous apologetic and ideological motives, would in this respect have found the present generation of scholars far more congenial.

There is perhaps no more laudatory eulogy to a deceased scholar than the studies that continue to honor his or her questions. And so the memory of Scholem is honored, for the questions he posed and the scheme of development of the Jewish mystical tradition that he suggested, especially as outlined in *Major Trends*, have remained the point of departure of all subsequent scholarship.[66]

Just months before Scholem was to publish *Major Trends in Jewish Mysticism*, he received notice that Walter Benjamin had died. In September 1940, fleeing Vichy France across the Spanish border, Benjamin was detained by the local police, and fearing that he would be returned to France and the German authorities, he took an overdose of morphine, putting an end to his life. Scholem dedicated

66 I wish to thank Rachel Elior for this observation. In February 1991, the Institut für Judaistik, Freie Universität Berlin, marked the fiftieth anniversary of the appearance of Scholem's *Major Trends* by sponsoring an international symposium, whose proceedings were published in P. Schaefer and J. Dan (eds.), *Major Trends in Jewish Mysticism: Fifty Years After*, Tübingen 1993. This enormously rich volume provides a comprehensive review of research developments in Jewish mysticism and Kabbala since the publication of *Major Trends* in 1941, with special emphasis on the directions of contemporary scholarship. The proceedings of a parallel conference exploring the wider impact of Scholem's life-work and legacy, also sponsored by the Institut für Judaistik, are to be published in M. Brocke, G. Smith, and P. Schaefer (eds.), *Scholem zwischen der Disziplinen*, Frankfurt a/M, in press.

his book to his beloved friend, 'whose genius united the insight of the Metaphysician, the interpretative power of the Critic and the erudition of the Scholar.' These words surely apply to Scholem himself.

GERSHOM SCHOLEM AND JUDAIC STUDIES

by

Ephraim E. Urbach

MORE THAN half a century has passed since Gershom Scholem initiated his life-long study of Jewish mysticism with the publication of his scholarly work on *Sefer ha-Bahir* (1923). In time, he became the foremost authority in the field he had founded and a central and dominant figure in Judaic Studies.

Scholem's views on the discipline of Judaic Studies, or what was known as *Wissenschaft des Judentums* (the Science of Judaism), and his opinions of its prominent representatives were presented in a series of articles devoted to this topic. This direct treatment, however, was a product of his inquiry into the sources that he studied, investigated and sought to understand. Scholem's was not an *a priori* critique of Judaic studies, based on programmatic statements and methodological declarations, but the outcome of exacting labor, sustained effort and the exercise of rare powers of perception. Thus, the first in his series of articles on this subject, the brilliant, ambitious and tempestuous 'Reflections on the Science of Judaism' (1944),[1] is preceded by 219 entries in the *Bibliography* of his writings; it postdates his *Major Trends in Jewish Mysticism* (1941) and his seminal essay 'Redemption through Sin' (1937).[2]

'Reflections on the Science of Judaism' encapsulates virtually all of Scholem's fundamental conceptual and methodological innovations in the study of Kabbala and messianism, as well as his views on the course of Jewish history, with all its tensions and complexities, its rises and falls. A close comparative reading of this essay together with 'Redemption through Sin' will serve us well, I believe, to

1 Reprinted in *Devarim be-go*, pp. 385–403.
2 *Messianic Idea*, pp. 78–141.

demonstrate Scholem's views on the nature of Judaic Studies and its place and role in history. Both articles are sharply critical, even condemnatory, in tone. Written with Scholem's unerring sense of style, each serves to illuminate the other. Although 'Redemption through Sin' is the earlier of the two and deals with an earlier historical period, I propose to discuss 'Reflections on the Science of Judaism' first, because, as we shall see, 'Redemption through Sin' is informed by the same concerns about the Science of Judaism that Scholem was to formulate expressly seven years later.

Scholem distinguishes three periods in the history of the Science of Judaism. The first began during the Emancipation period, when the primary aspiration of many Jews was to rid themselves of the confines imposed by their distinctiveness and to assimilate within the nations among whom they lived. The Jewish Enlightenment (the *Haskala*) was rife with trends leading in the direction of the historical suicide of Judaism, its liquidation and breakdown. Scholem's claim is that the *Wissenschaft* scholars shared this self-destructive tendency. In its earliest period, the remarkable adventure of the Science of Judaism embodied a basic and profound inner contradiction between its conservative and destructive elements. As Scholem ironically emphasized, the studies in Judaism conducted by its outstanding representatives at the time — particularly Leopold Zunz and Moritz Steinschneider, whose talents, achievements and personalities Scholem greatly admired — were just what Steinschneider himself had called them: a 'decent burial' for Judaism.

The main thrust of Scholem's critique, however, is directed at the second period of the Science of Judaism, when it had achieved scholarly respectability and influence over Western Jewry by appearing in a version congenial to bourgeois society and serving its ends. The dialectic tension had dissipated. Research into the history of Jewish martyrs or about the great scholars of Judaism, who had disseminated enlightenment in their time, gave a sense of pride to a generation that had no intention of following these historical examples, but awaited instead the messiah of liberalism. This mixture of sentimentality and apologetics — together with the suppression of 'undesirable' documents, thus removing the irrationalist sting from the history of Judaism and muffling its mystic fervor — emerged triumphant

30

in the Science of Judaism. Scholem rejects the Hebrew poet H.N. Bialik's attempt to blame estrangement from the Hebrew language for this situation. He claims that there was no difference between Enlightenment scholars who favored Hebrew and those who wrote in other languages. Scholem acknowledges that some of the scholars of the period were giants of erudition, but as independent thinkers they were midgets. He says of David Kaufmann: 'He was brilliantly talented, and there were few of his caliber in his generation or ours,' but at the same time he also asserts that his works embody some of the worst tendencies of romantic scholarship, 'a feeble, sentimental and sanctimonious love.' According to Scholem, not a single original, non-ossified word concerning the Jewish religion issued from this circle in fifty years, from 1850 to 1900. These scholars almost completely neglected the subject of *halakha* (Jewish religious law) as a study in concrete religious issues rather than a matter of literary history; as a religious issue it figured not at all.

The third period of the Science of Judaism began with the Jewish nationalist movement. The perspective changed: the slogan now was that Judaism must be viewed from within; the entire scientific edifice must be reconstructed in the light of the collective Jewish historical experience. For this new critical structure, a general change in orientation was not sufficient: it was necessary to re-examine every detail, to reappraise each problem on a fundamental level. Although the method was to be uncompromisingly scientific in its criteria, like the work of Zunz and Steinschneider, its motivating force was to be positive and constructive. The quest for the light of scientific truth in its ideal form could succeed only through intimate knowledge of the individual details, yet appreciation of the power of facts must be tempered by the realization that 'nothing is more misleading than fact.' This was the new scholarly vision. But what was the reality? Scholem concludes his 'Reflections on the Science of Judaism' in the same pessimistic spirit with which he opened:

> We have stalled on the road from the vision to its realization. We sought to rebel but found ourselves continuing tradition instead. Sentimentality wears a new garb no less irritating than its former guise. The defects now wear national dress. In short, the Science of Judaism needs to be overhauled from top to bottom.

At first reading, the section delineating the earlier periods of the Science of Judaism seems well-founded and objective, while Scholem's assessment of the third period seems no more than a statement of his hopes and concerns, for he gives no detailed explanation for the change in perspective resulting from the renascence of the nationalist movement. In fact, the opposite is true. An examination of the sources reveals that Scholem overstated the case concerning the scholars of destruction of the first period and exaggerated in his disparagement of the second period as an 'orgy of mediocrity.' But he was to correct his own error, a characteristic of his scholarship to which he later attributed much of his success.[3]

In a lecture delivered in London in 1959 entitled 'The Science of Judaism — Then and Now,'[4] Scholem was more moderate and restrained. While critical of the tendency to reduce Judaism to an abstract, spiritualized phenomenon, which, he argued, meant censoring the Jewish past, he nevertheless describes those against whom he leveled this charge as 'eminent scholars and great personalities, [who] have left us all a great and positive heritage for which each of us can never be sufficiently grateful.' The defects in their scholarship were attributable, in Scholem's view, to the socio-political milieu in which they worked. He even admits that the romantic enthusiasm which he so vehemently rejects 'overcomes their original proclivity to liquidate, spiritualize and de-actualize Judaism. It drives them on to positive insights far removed from what they originally envisioned.'[5] Scholem even finds a justification and objective for their apologetics in the circumstances of their time. None of this, to be sure, forestalls his criticism of the defects and shortcomings in their work and of the deliberate omissions ensuing from their hostility or disparagement; but all these are by way of emphasis of the main point, which is the significance of the change

---

3 *Devarim be-go*, p. 65.
4 First published as 'Wissenschaft vom Judentum einst und jetzt,' *Bulletin für Mitglieder der Gesellschaft der Freunde des Leo Baeck Institute*, III (1960); included in *Messianic Idea*, pp. 304–313. See also E.E. Urbach, 'Contemporary Judaic Studies — Status and Problems,' *Proceedings of the Sixth World Congress of Judaic Studies*, I, Jerusalem 1977, p. 25, note 11.
5 *Messianic Idea*, p. 307.

in perspective ushered in by the movement of national rebirth, Zionism. The Zionist movement — 'in agreement,' Scholem adds, 'with Zunz's view at the very beginning' — once more saw Judaism as a living organism and not merely as an idea, and could therefore 'apply criteria of values entirely different from those of a purely philosophical and theological view of what Judaism represented as a historical phenomenon.'

Had this turning point, which began with the emergence of Zionism, had an effect on Judaic Studies? Scholem correctly avers that with the exception of a few Zionist scholars, the first twenty or thirty years of the movement's existence had no perceptible impact upon the scholarly perspective. While he does not say so openly, it is clear that the one scholar who was fully alert to the possibilities inherent in this change, and the only one to have given it significant expression, was none other than Gershom Scholem. The problem of Judaic Studies, for him, brooked no evasion. 'This problem,' he states, 'is of immanent significance for us; it burns in our souls.' Using the plural, Scholem spoke for himself. But if the problem could not be avoided, confronting it was vital to the discipline. Despite the great difficulties involved, there must be an effort to arrive at a full picture of the functioning of the Jewish organism in relation to the real world surrounding it: 'We must determine on which of the various levels, from the most refined to the most despised, there existed a vital intercourse — whether or not we happen to like it.'[6]

In order to comprehend the significance of Scholem's position, let us turn to his essay, 'Redemption through Sin,'[7] which is devoted to what most consider one of the most 'despised' chapters of our history, the Sabbatean movement subsequent to Sabbetai Zevi's conversion to Islam. The need to view Jewish history from a new, national, non-assimilationist perspective opened Scholem's eyes to stirrings of redemption in phenomena that the sober Jewish citizen of the last century viewed as a nightmarish aberration.

6 *Ibid.*, p. 309.
7 Scholem declares in the introduction to his anthology *Mehqarim u-meqorot shel ha-shabbeta'ut ve-gilguleha* (Jerusalem 1974): 'On the whole, I still maintain these points of view, although there is much to add and clarify.'

33

Sabbetai Zevi's followers subsequent to his conversion were not charlatans but sincere, if naive, believers. This applies as well to the adherents of Jacob Frank, who was, in Scholem's words, 'one of the most frightening phenomena in Jewish history, a religious leader who was in all his actions a truly corrupt and degenerate individual.' This situation demands an explanation, which Scholem offers as he leads us from the lowest and most simple to the highest, most complex strata of the structure of Jewish society and thought.

The messianic idea took on new stripes in the Lurianic Kabbala, which transformed it into a cosmic drama. 'A contradiction developed between the two levels of the drama of redemption, that of the subjective experience of the individual on the one hand, and that of the objective historical facts on the other.'[8] Post-conversion Sabbateanism was born when large segments of Jewish society refused to submit to the sentence of history by admitting that their own personal experience had been false and untrustworthy. With a new sense of life provided by the power of their belief in 'the restored world,' the Sabbateans, particularly the extremists, developed an image of themselves as elect 'pneumatics,' set apart from others who did not partake of supreme illumination. This sense of superiority, the pretension to be the vanguard of a new world, led them to throw off the restraints of religious law and become rebels.

The ecstasy of the 'spiritual elite' poses problems for traditional, normative religion, which frequently has a 'bourgeios' tone. In the history of Christianity and Islam, that tension has often erupted into full-blown conflict. Medieval Judaism had the power to curb most of its ecstatics, but Sabbateanism caused an explosion. It took the form of a sect whose members all belonged to the 'spiritual elite' and carried its basic assumptions to their ultimate conclusions. Whereas Hasidism, knowing the secret of 'thus far shalt thou come, but no further,' forced ecstatics to curb their unruly spirituality, the Sabbateans 'pressed on to the end, into the abyss of the mythical gates of impurity, where pure spiritual awareness of a world made new became a pitfall fraught with peril for the moral life.'[9]

8 *Messianic Idea*, p. 88.
9 *Ibid.*, p. 91.

34

Sabbateans believed that 'the Messiah is constrained to commit "strange acts," of which his apostasy is the most startling.' The messiah's act is not a transgression, but the fulfillment of a commandment, 'a commandment fulfilled by means of a transgression' — a traditional idea appearing in an altered sense. Through such dialectic audacity, the Sabbateans transformed the content of Judaism into a Gnostic heresy.[10] 'When one considers how wildly extravagant all this may appear even now, it is easy enough to appreciate the wrath and indignation with which such a theology was greeted by the orthodox camp in its own day,' wrote Scholem. Nonetheless, he finds an authentically Jewish will 'in these paradoxical individuals too, in their desire to start afresh and their realization of the fact that negating the exile meant negating its religious and institutional forms as well and returning to the original fountainheads of the Jewish faith. This last practice — a tendency to rely in matters of belief upon the Bible and the Aggada — grew to be particularly strong among the nihilists in the movement.'[11]

While moderate Sabbateanism preserved traditional Jewish practice, it completely overturned the inner world of historic Judaism. As Scholem states, 'we can nevertheless rely on the judgment of those anti-Sabbatean polemicists who saw perfectly clearly that the inward devastation of old values was no less dangerous or far-reaching than its outward manifestation.'[12]

Scholem places in its proper context within the history of religions the doctrine of the holiness of sin propounded by the radical Sabbateans, who transformed messianism into nihilism, abandoning

---

10 As noted by Julius Guttmann, Nahman Krochmal (1785–1840) pointed out the connection between Sabbateanism and Gnosticism in *More nevukhe ha-zeman* (ed. D. Rawidowicz, Jerusalem 1953, p. 271); see J. Guttmann, *Philosophies of Judaism*, p. 391. (In the 1933 German edition of Guttmann's book, Krochmal was mentioned only briefly, on p. 319: the later English version is indicative of the change in perspective of which Scholem spoke.) See also Scholem's remarks in his article 'Religious Authority and Mysticism,' in *Kabbalah and Symbolism*, pp. 23f. Scholem considered Krochmal 'exceptional' among Wissenschaft scholars; see 'Reflections on the Science of Judaism,' *Devarim be-go*, p. 389.

11 *Messianic Idea*, p. 106.

12 *Ibid.*, p. 108.

not only their messiah but themselves as well to religious anarchy. He characterizes them as a spiritualist sect claiming to represent the world of a spiritual elite, which, in their view, differed completely from that of ordinary people. A member of the spiritual elite acted according to a different standard and could not be judged by accepted moral norms. Aspirations of this kind had always existed in the Kabbala *in potentia*, but never in practice. When the Sabbateans joined the concepts of the 'Torah of Emanation' (*tora de-'azilut*) and 'Torah of Formation' (*tora de-beri'a*),[13] employed by the Kabbalists of Safed, with the doctrine of the 'cosmic aeons' (*shemittot*), they transformed them into slogans of a new nihilistic morality. Transgressions were sanctified: perverted sexual desires found an ideological justification. Scholem emphasizes 'the accuracy of the charges leveled against the Sabbateans, based on the evidence of their "confessions" which have come down to us in both theological and homiletical form.'[14]

Scholem explains the nihilistic attitude towards the entire structure of *tora de-beri'a* as 'an expression of the desire for renewal, which came to nought for lack of suitable conditions under which to function.' The desire to negate and devalue the Jewish historical order was one of the strongest factors in the development of the nihilistic mentality. The radicals of the movement had no political program; their way of revitalizing national life was by trampling its guiding principles underfoot. This led them down dark byways, which terminated in their support of the like of Jacob Frank. But even here, Scholem does not forgo an explanation of the satanic power exercised by the iniquities of this unscrupulous adventurer. He finds in Frank's territorialist program a bizarre expression of his followers' longings for a reconstitution of Jewish life, and even for productivization. In the published sections of Frank's writings, which few have bothered to read, Scholem discovers a decided talent for 'the pithy, the strikingly illustrative and the concretely symbolic expression.'[15] Frank's nihilism contained a religious mythology

13 *Ibid.*, p. 111.
14 *Ibid.*, p. 114.
15 *Ibid.*, p. 128.

similar to that of the nihilistic Gnostics of the second century. It is not, however, the particular brand of mythology that is of primary interest, but the fact that it could have been created at this time and place, and been accepted by sizable numbers of ghetto Jews as a new tiding. This was an indicator of the internal disintegration of the Jewish world.

The desire to abolish all the old laws and conventions was renewed, according to Scholem, with the French Revolution. In the wake of this upheaval, the last Sabbateans opened their hearts to the spirit of the *Haskala*, 'assimilation accomplishing without paradox, indeed without religion at all, what the members of the "accursed sect" had earnestly striven for in a stormy contention with truth, carried on in the half light of a faith pregnant with paradoxes.'[16]

'Redemption through Sin' is a model of that kind of research which joins wide-ranging and brilliant insights with a close examination of details, none of which are condemned to exclusion or derision. The point at which 'Redemption through Sin' ends, the entry into the world of the *Haskala* and secularism, marks the starting point of Scholem's reflections on Jewish *Wissenschaft*, which served as a weapon in the battle of the *Haskala* for internal and external emancipation.

By virtue of his analysis of the chaotic world of Sabbateanism, Gershom Scholem was able as well to point the way to a renewal of the discipline of Judaic Studies, which itself became an integral part of the historical process under consideration. This created problems and contradictions, and it continues to present us with challenges and opportunities, as well as obstacles of which we must be aware. Precisely because of his cognizance of the change in perspective brought about by the Zionist movement, Scholem warns of the dangers of a one-sided perception of Jewish history based solely on the Zionist point of view. He repeatedly voices his fear of reverse apologetics, which would impose a Zionist interpretation on all the phenomena under study.

At a 1970 colloquium on '*Wissenschaft des Judentums* in Germany and Its Influence on Modern Research,'[17] Scholem responded to the

16 *Ibid.*, p. 141.
17 This colloquium, chaired by Ephraim E. Urbach, took place in the framework

question of whether there is a unity to Jewish history, or whether it is to be perceived, rather, as a series of episodes to be interpreted independently within the context of general history. Scholem's position was that, 'from our understanding and personal experience,' he tended towards a 'holistic view' of the history of the Jewish people. He did not expand upon this 'holistic view,' but in light of his allusion to 'personal experience,' let us refer to an autobiographical statement given in an interview with Muki Tzur in 1974:

> I have always considered secular Zionism a legitimate way, but rejected the foolish declaration about the Jews becoming 'a nation like all the other nations.'... I cannot free myself of the dialectical lesson of history, according to which secularism is part of the process of our entry into history; entry into history means assimilating into it. Since I do not believe in our becoming 'like all the other nations,' I do not see secularism as a possibility, and it will not come to pass.[18]

Scholem's exemplary use of the phenomenological method to shed light on religious phenomena went hand in hand with his own independent religious thought; it suffices to mention his remarks concerning Jewish theology today, and his sensitivity to living faith, which he expressed emphatically in his interview with Tzur:

> I have never cut myself off from God. I don't understand atheists; I never did. ... I think atheism is understandable only if you accept the rule of unbridled passions, a life without values. ... I am convinced that there is no morality that has inner meaning unless it has a religious basis. I don't believe there is such a thing as the absolute autonomy of man, whereby man makes himself and the world creates itself.

of a symposium held in Jerusalem on 'Perspectives of German-Jewish History in the 19th and 20th Century,' sponsored by the Leo Baeck Institute. The proceedings were published in a book by the same title (Jerusalem 1971, English and German editions).

18 *On Jews and Judaism in Crisis*, New York 1976, pp. 34–35 (quoted here with slight revisions). On the meaning of 'generational continuity' see E.E. Urbach, '*'Al Gershom Shalom*,' *Molad*, N.S. I (1968), p. 437 (in Hebrew).

Scholem's vast contribution to Judaic Studies surpasses his numerous and significant works of research, and the solutions he posed to the problems presented in them. A revitalizing spirit issues from everything he wrote and created, reaching out beyond his own major field of interest to challenge those engaged in other areas of Judaic Studies as well. It demands that they delve into previously unformulated questions and problems, and indicates new directions of research inherent in the sources they study. Scholem's legacy sends out rays of light over a wide variety of subjects; the brilliant sparks borne within it illuminate a host of topics ranging back through the Jewish past.

GERSHOM SCHOLEM'S CONTRIBUTION TO THE STUDY OF THE *ZOHAR*

by

Isaiah Tishby

THE STUDY of the *Zohar* had a unique significance in the life of Gershom Scholem, and it figured prominently throughout his sixty years of unbroken scholarly activity. Scholem's description of his first youthful encounter with the major work of pre-Lurianic Kabbala, recounted in his memoir, *From Berlin to Jerusalem*, provides some of that book's most fascinating reading.

At age fourteen, the youthful Gerhard Scholem was in revolt against the spirit of assimilation dominating his family home in Berlin. Influenced by the nineteenth-century *Wissenschaft* scholar Heinrich Graetz's history of the Jews, which had come into his hands by chance, he was attracted to Judaism and set out to discover more about it. His path, however, was strewn with difficulties. He turned initially to the Orthodox Jewish community, but its beliefs and way of life did not appeal to him. In Graetz's work, he had read about the existence and history of Jewish mysticism, and about the reverence of the kabbalists for the holy book of the *Zohar*. Graetz described the *Zohar*'s doctrine as obscure gibberish, and the work itself as a 'book of lies,' written by the plagiarist Moses de Leon, a thirteenth-century kabbalist who, for personal gain, had attributed it to Rabbi Simeon bar Yohai and his colleagues of the mishnaic period. Scholem, however, intuitively sensed that hidden within the maligned *Zohar* lay the key to a different kind of Judaism, more vital than what he had hitherto encountered.

Although he longed to study the book in the original, its Aramaic and its bizarre, complex style remained impenetrable to him even after he had learned Hebrew and had begun reading other source texts and secondary studies on Kabbala and Hasidism. When his

40

teacher of Talmud and rabbinic literature confessed that he, too, was unable to understand the *Zohar*, Scholem saw no alternative to making his way through it by himself. He succeeded so well that he had already begun teaching the *Zohar* to his friends before he immigrated to Palestine in 1923.

Scholem prepared himself for scholarly research on the *Zohar* during the course of his doctoral studies, which culminated in his dissertation on the *Sefer Bahir*, one of the oldest and most problematic kabbalistic works. After he settled in Jerusalem, the *Zohar* became a major focus of his research. He devoted his 1925 inaugural lecture in Kabbala at the Institute for Jewish Studies to the question, 'Did Moses de Leon Write the *Zohar*?'[1] Even before this, in a programmatic letter to the Hebrew poet Hayyim Nahman Bialik in the summer of 1925, Scholem designated the solution of the problems posed by the *Zohar* as one of the major and most pressing objectives of Kabbala studies.[2] He set himself an extraordinarily broad range of scholarly tasks in that letter, and of the four large projects enumerated under the heading 'Substantive Studies,' two are 'An Introduction to the *Zohar*' and a 'Lexicon of the *Zohar*.' The Lexicon was already partially complete at the time, and he continued to work on it until the end of his life.

Scholem's *Zohar* scholarship was of two kinds: (1) *Zohar* criticism, whose principal goal is to determine the time of the *Zohar*'s composition and the identity of its author; and (2) clarification of the *Zohar*'s ideational system and its place in the history of Jewish mysticism. I dealt with Scholem's critical studies of the *Zohar* in *The Wisdom of the Zohar*,[3] and many of his major innovations, both general and specific, are described there and compared with the assertions of his predecessors. For present purposes, a brief survey of his central conclusions, as presented in chapter 5 of Scholem's *Major Trends in Jewish Mysticism*, will suffice: (1) Moses de Leon was the author of all parts of the *Zohar*, except for the *Ra'aya mehemana* and *Tiqqunei zohar*, which were written by an anonymous kabbalist,

1 Published in *Mada'ei ha-yahadut*, I (1925/6), pp. 16–29.
2 Reprinted in *Devarim be-go*, pp. 59–63.
3 I. Tishby, *The Wisdom of the Zohar*, Oxford 1989, 3 vols. (translation from the Hebrew *Mishnat ha-zohar*, Jerusalem 1948/9).

apparently of Moses de Leon's circle. (2) The *Midrash ha-ne'lam*, written in a mixture of Hebrew and Aramaic and full of Tibbonite philosophical terminology, is the earliest part of the *Zohar*. (3) Moses de Leon wrote the greater part of his pseudepigraphic work before his Hebrew compositions, which bear dates from 1286 through 1293. (4) The *Midrash ha-ne'lam* was written before 1280, the other sections of the *Zohar* between 1280 and 1286. (5) The zoharic terms cited in de Leon's Hebrew works, with allusions to their antiquity and importance, show that they were intended to prepare the ground for the dissemination of the *Zohar* as an ancient work — a task that engaged Moses de Leon from 1293, the year in which he finished his last Hebrew work, until his death in 1305. In concluding my chapter on 'The History of the Study of the *Zohar*,' I stated:

> There is no doubt that Scholem's critical conclusions have finally put an end to the great controversy about the composition and authorship of the *Zohar* that raged for many years among students of Judaism.[4]

In the following pages, I would like to focus on Scholem's studies of the *Zohar*'s mystical scheme and his conclusions regarding its nature and significance.

The Kabbala of the Zohar and the 'Gnostic Kabbala' of the Thirteenth Century

Like the rest of *Major Trends in Jewish Mysticism*, the condensed summary of the *Zohar*'s kabbalistic doctrine in chapter 6 is based on Scholem's 1938 lecture series in New York. In the fifteen years that had passed since the publication of his first article on Moses de Leon, Scholem had published additional studies in *Zohar* criticism, but none about its doctrine. The entry 'Kabbala' in the German-language *Encyclopedia Judaica*[5] presented kabbalistic doctrines thematically and did not deal explicitly with their historical development, treating those of the *Zohar* only within the general context of the Spanish Kabbala. An exception is Scholem's 1935

---

4 *Ibid.*, I, p. 55.
5 Berlin 1932, IX, cols. 630–732.

introduction to a German translation of the first portions of the *Zohar*, containing the interpretation of Creation.[6] One chapter of the introduction, entitled 'Towards a Substantive Understanding of the Zohar,' discusses the doctrine of the Godhead and the symbols of the ten *sefirot*, while the preceding chapter deals with *Zohar* criticism. Together they form a preliminary version of the more extensive discussion in *Major Trends*.

Scholem thus wrote a summary of the doctrines of the *Zohar* before publishing any detailed and specific studies, and that he should do so in connection with so broad and central a topic calls for explanation. I believe that this procedure was dictated by the course taken by his research into the *Zohar*, which had been one of his main preoccupations since the beginning of his scholarly career. In his first article, mentioned above, Scholem set out to challenge Graetz's assertion that Moses de Leon was the author of the *Zohar*. Scholem's counter-hypothesis was that the *Zohar* was a collection of 'fragments from earlier periods' assembled by de Leon and his thirteenth-century Spanish circle of kabbalists. However, Scholem gradually realized that this view was incorrect. As he states at the end of the expanded Hebrew edition of his memoirs, published a few days after his death: 'I devoted the next ten to fifteen years to this study [i.e., to disproving the view that Moses de Leon was the author of the *Zohar*], and one by one I refuted the arguments presented in my inaugural lecture, although I had set out to buttress them.'[7]

The error proved most fruitful, for in his attempts to verify his thesis, Scholem made solid advances in his research. These scholarly achievements, apart from their importance in themselves, served as the cornerstones for his mature and comprehensive overview of *Zohar* criticism and zoharic doctrine. Moreover, it was here that Scholem first demonstrated his phenomenal ability to bring a wide range of disciplines simultaneously to bear upon his research, including philology, bio-bibliography, mythology, the history of

6 G. Scholem, *Die Geheimnisse der Schöpfung — Ein Kapitel aus dem Sohar*, Berlin 1935.

7 *Mi-berlin lirushalayim*, Jerusalem 1981, p. 224 (in Hebrew).

ideas and more. I refer to his seminal studies of the obscure thought and complex imagery in the forgotten works of the brothers Jacob and Isaac Ha-kohen and their circle of late thirteenth-century Castilian kabbalists, whose doctrines Scholem characterized as 'Gnostic Kabbala.'

Scholem's first book-length study of these kabbalists was published in 1925/6,[8] shortly after the appearance of his first article on *Zohar* criticism. One motive, perhaps the principal one, for this study was undoubtedly Scholem's desire to buttress the hypothesis presented in his debut lecture; the study's subtitle is 'Sources for the History of the Kabbala before the Appearance of the *Zohar*,' and the central chapter deals with some doctrines common to the *Zohar* and the writings of Isaac Ha-kohen. Scholem then published, between 1931 and 1934, a series of studies that were brought together in a volume entitled 'A Study of the Kabbala of R. Isaac Ha-kohen.'[9] Written just when Scholem was in the midst of revising his views about the connection between Moses de Leon and the *Zohar*, this volume provides interesting indications of the process of his retreat from his earlier hypothesis. Of particular note in this connection is his chapter on the nature and varied meanings of the four worlds of *azilut, beri'a, yezira* and *'assiya* (emanation, creation, formation and making) in the *Zohar*, in Moses de Leon's Hebrew writings, and in the *Ra'aya mehemana* and *Tiqqunei zohar*.[10]

These studies are highly significant for their indications of the changes that took place in Scholem's understanding of the mystical doctrines of the *Zohar*, during those years when he restricted himself in his published works to *Zohar* criticism. Scholem realized from the very beginning that the *Zohar*'s doctrine was mythic-Gnostic. Indeed, that was what drew him to it; the mythologization of Judaism fascinated him, and he sensed its vitalizing power. Already in 1919, when he changed his course of university studies from mathematics to Judaic studies in order to study the Kabbala, it was the allure

8 Mada'ei ha-yahadut, II (1925/6), pp. 103–293 (in Hebrew).
9 *Le-heqer kabbalat R. Yitzhaq ben Ya'aqov ha-kohen*, Jerusalem 1934 (in Hebrew).
10 *Ibid.*, 'The Development of the the Doctrine of the Worlds in the Early Kabbala.'

of mythic-Gnostic thought that determined his choice of the *Sefer ha-bahir* as the topic of his dissertation. Scholem kept returning to the *Bahir* throughout his career, for he regarded that fragmented pseudepigraphic pamphlet, the earliest kabbalistic work that has come down to us, as the repository of the broken links between the early Kabbala and ancient Gnostic trends within Judaism and outside it. Scholem's earliest research, in which he still maintained his hypothesis that the *Zohar* was constructed of 'fragments from early times,' led him to hope and believe that its mythology might have roots reaching back to the first centuries C.E. He even toyed with the notion that these ideas might have some connection with the development of non-Jewish Gnosis. However, since he had not yet proven his hypothesis about the early origins of the *Zohar*, and indeed became convinced over the years that his position was untenable, Scholem resolved not to make pronouncements about the mystical doctrines of the *Zohar* before formulating his conclusions concerning its authorship.

Scholem's final position, that the mythical elements in the *Zohar* are a product of thirteenth-century Spanish Kabbala, led him to revise thoroughly his analysis of the *Zohar*'s place in the history of the Kabbala, and above all his assessment of the relationship between the *Zohar* and the 'Gnostic Kabbala' of the Castilian circle. The documents produced by the Castilians are replete with references to sources of various kinds, most of them pseudepigraphic, some of which are said to derive from the East. Scholem had originally thought that the affinity between the mythology and demonology of the Castilian works and those of the *Zohar* stemmed from their use of a shared or similiar corpus of Hellenistic-Oriental sources. However, once he concluded that the Zohar was entirely the original work of Moses de Leon, he re-evaluated the concepts introduced by the 'Gnostic Kabbala,' posing a critical new understanding of the sources of the Zohar and its unique character.

From the beginning, Scholem had regarded the Ha-kohen brothers' doctrine as a 'Gnostic reaction' against the philosophization of the Kabbala characteristic of the school of Isaac the Blind, and especially of the thought of Azriel of Gerona. At the earliest stage of his research, Scholem assumed that it was their oft-quoted sources

45

from the East that had influenced the Castilian circle's reaction against the imposition of Neoplatonic concepts on the mythic-Gnostic imagery of the *Bahir*. Simultaneously with the change in his position regarding the authorship of the *Zohar*, he arrived at the conclusion that the mythic reversal of the 'Gnostic Kabbala' was in fact the spontaneous internal development of its own inventiveness, and that the author of the *Zohar*, though he added much of his own, was directly influenced by this school. But the *Zohar*, alongside its mythic-Gnostic aspect, is also strikingly characterized by ideas deriving from the Neoplatonic version of philosophical Kabbala. Scholem's final assessment of the *Zohar*'s doctrine was that it fused the two main, opposing streams of Spanish Kabbala: the speculative system of the disciples of Isaac the Blind in Gerona, and the Gnostic vision of the Ha-kohen brothers and their Castilian followers.

The Doctrine of the Zohar

Scholem's fully formed analysis of the *Zohar*'s doctrine in *Major Trends* rests upon this new understanding of its synthetic nature. According to Scholem, Moses de Leon erected a unique new structure on the foundation of two kabbalistic traditions, the one speculative and philosophical, the other based on tangible imagery. His bold innovativeness, which tended to the figurative and mythic, burst existing boundaries and pressed its mark even upon his borrowed sources, giving them an entirely new visage.

Scholem begins by noting features of the *Zohar*'s doctrine that distinguish it from other systems of thought, including the contemporary prophetic mysticism of Abraham Abulafia, the rationalist Jewish philosophy of the Middle Ages, and ancient *merkava* mysticism. The *Zohar*'s chief concern with the mysteries of the divine world is as an object of mystical contemplation, not as a guide for ecstatic mystical experience. The author of the *Zohar* does not speak in the language of an elite, but rather expresses the emotions and fears of ordinary people. Unlike the philosophers, who challenged the simple faith of the people, mystics of the type represented by the *Zohar*'s author saw and presented their views of the Godhead as fully in keeping with traditional beliefs about the God of creation and revelation. The *Zohar* casts its mysteries into homiletic expansions on the scriptural text rather than systematic expositions, and this form of expression was instrumental in imparting its ideas to a wide public.

Scholem calls the Kabbala of the *Zohar* a Jewish theosophy, 'a mystical doctrine ... which purports to perceive and to describe the mysterious workings of the Divinity, perhaps also believing it possible to become absorbed in its contemplation.'[11] This kind of theosophy postulates that there is 'a kind of divine emanation whereby God, abandoning his self-contained repose, awakens to mysterious life,' and that 'the mysteries of creation reflect the pulsation of this divine life.'[12]

In order to illustrate some of the unique characteristics of the *Zohar*'s theosophical system, let us examine two of its major themes as interpreted by Scholem: the mystery of the Godhead, including the hidden God (*'Ein-Sof*) and the revealed God (*sefirot*); and the mystical 'Nothingness' (*'ayin*), i.e., the *Zohar*'s doctrine of *creatio ex nihilo*.

(a) The Mystery of the Godhead

'Ein-Sof, the hidden God, has neither qualities nor attributes, but from within His hidden being are manifested powers that form an order of ten *sefirot*. The manifest God and the hidden God, the *sefirot* and *'Ein-Sof*, are integrally united, like flame and coal, and the complete existence of the divine Being consists in their unity. The *sefirot* were formed by a process of emanation. They are active in creation and in the direction of the world, but, unlike the tripartite Neoplatonic emanations (intelligence, soul, nature), they are considered part of the divine Being, not intermediary stages or bridges between the divine and the cosmos.

The *sefirot* are reflected and apprehensible in all realms of reality via concrete symbols. The symbolic aspects of the *sefirot* are unlimited, in both the spiritual and the material realms. However, the symbols are not allegorical representations, which have no existence in the divine realm they symbolize; on the contrary, their real existence is within the system of divine powers, and the things

11 *Major Trends*, p. 206.
12 *Ibid.*

that serve as means of symbolization are images of the concealed supernal reality.

The *Zohar* depicts the world of the *sefirot* as a mystical organism, using symbols that serve to depict the entire system. Two such frequently used symbols are *ilan ha-'azilut* ('the tree of emanation'), and *demut ha-'adam* ('the image of man'). The 'tree of emanation' symbolizes the entire Godhead; it is rooted in *'Ein-Sof*, the source of all, and the *sefirot* are its branches. But the supernal entity symbolized by the tree is also the entire cosmos, for all created beings are outgrowths, as it were, of the divine branches, sustained and quickened by the divine plenitude flowing down into them. A similar dual relation between the symbol and what it represents pertains to the 'image of man,' which the *Zohar* describes in detail, all parts of the human body constituting symbolic representations of parts of the divine Being. Here, too, the image of man is not only a figurative vehicle for mystical contemplation of the Godhead; each limb and organ of the human body is actually suffused with and activated by the divine force of the *sefira* it represents.

The mythic elements of this anthropomorphic symbolism are radically expressed via sexual imagery. Unlike most non-Jewish mystical streams, the *Zohar* refrains from using erotic imagery to describe the relationship between the soul and God, but it is extravagant in the use of such imagery to depict the life of the Godhead itself. Two human images are operative in this symbolic framework: that of the upper *sefirot*, symbolized by the male image, and that of the tenth *sefira*, the *Shekhina*, represented as the female image. The *Zohar* refers frequently to the sacred union within the Godhead, from which flows the divine plenitude that begets and sustains the world. Erotic episodes of various kinds are described in great detail, as the most holy and exalted of mysteries.

Graetz and other rationalist scholars denounced this imagery as sacrilegious. Scholem, however, argued that they 'misconstrue both the morality and the tendency of the Zohar ... but above all they completely ignore the problem presented by the resurrection of mythology in the heart of mystical Judaism, of which the *Zohar* is the classical representative.'[13] Even those scholars who did not

---

13 *Major Trends*, p. 228.

view the mythologization of Judaism as a vitalizing religious factor, charged Scholem, should have been moved to wonder why such 'abominations' were accepted by broad circles within Judaism, and were even introduced into its liturgy and religious rituals; rather than denouncing the revival of myth, they should have sought explanations for its powerful influence.

(b) Creation from Nothing (beri'a yesh mi-'ayin)

The concept of the mystical Nothing occupies an important place in the *Zohar's* theosophy and doctrine of creation. In mystical terms, the primal act of creation out of nothing is paradoxically, the self-creation of God, the crisis of the *Ein Sof*'s emergence from eternal repose to manifest His power in the dynamic system of the *sefirot*. The first phase of this event is the contraction of the hidden, infinite God into Nothing (*'ayin*), which is the first *sefira*, *Keter 'Elyon* ('supreme crown'). The second *sefira*, *Hokhma* or the 'wisdom of God,' emanates from this act, constituting the first divine being or entity (*yesh*), symbolized by a point; the emanation of *Hokhma* from *Keter* is thus the emergence of being (*yesh*) from Nothing (*'ayin*). A succession of divine beings extends from *hokhma*, ending with the emanation of the *sefira* of *malkhut*, the *Shekhina*, one of whose symbolic representations is 'I' (*'ani*). The anagrammatic play on the words *'ayin* and *'ani*[14] expresses the dialectical transformation of the divine and inapprehensible Nothing into the divine 'I,' an object of contemplation. The power of this divine 'I' created the non-divine worlds, which are sparks of the *sefirot*, existing by virtue of their divine origins and serving symbolically to mirror them.

The *Zohar* explicates its concept of creation as the self-creation of the Godhead by means of a bold exegesis of the Hebrew word-order of the opening phrase of the Bible ('In the beginning God created'), which the *Zohar* interprets as referring to the emanation of the first three *sefirot*.[15] A similar method is used to explain the formation of the seven lower *sefirot*, which complete the Godhead:

---

14 *'ayin* = 'alef, yud, nun; *'ani* = 'alef, nun, yud.

15 *Bereshit bara 'elohim* — i.e., it was by means of the second *sefira*, called *reshit* (= *hokhma*), that the first *sefira*, the Nothing (the unnamed subject of the verse), emanated the third *sefira*, called *'elohim* (= *bina*).

the *Zohar*'s account again rests on an esoteric exegesis of a biblical reference to creation, in Isaiah 40:26: 'Lift up your eyes on high and behold who has created these?'[16] This unique type of exegesis served to demonstrate the *Zohar*'s contention that Scripture is full of kabbalistic secrets. To quote Scholem: 'These are only a few instances of the method by which the author of the *Zohar* seeks to describe in symbolical terms the theosophical universe of God's hidden life.'[17]

The Place of the Zohar in Jewish Mysticism

Scholem's study of the doctrines of the *Zohar* seems, on the face of it, to conclude with the publication of *Major Trends* in 1941. The bibliography of his works lists no later study specifically on the *Zohar*, aside from encyclopedia articles, a selection from the *Zohar* in English translation (1949), and an article on *Zohar* criticism.[18]

In reality, however, Scholem's 1949 lecture on 'Kabbala and Myth,' the first of a series of lectures on various topics in Jewish mysticism, opened a new and extremely important phase in his study of the Kabbala of the *Zohar*: an examination of its doctrines within broad historical frameworks, extending from pre-kabbalistic sources to late offshoots of the Kabbala. All of these studies have been published in various frameworks, and many of them have been brought together in English translation.[19]

16 *Mi bara 'ele* — i.e., the third *sefira*, *bina*, called *mi*, is the supernal mother who gave birth to the seven lower *sefirot* from *hesed* to *malkhut*, referred to as *'ele*. Putting together the letters of the words *mi* and *'ele* yields the word *'elohim* (God), demonstrating that this process completes the self-creation of the Godhead.
17 *Major Trends*, p. 221.
18 'A New Chapter of *Midrash ha-ne'elam*,' *Ginzberg Jubilee Volume*, New York 1945/6 (in Hebrew).
19 Most of these lectures were given within the framework of the Eranos conferences in Ascona and published in German in the volumes of the *Eranos Jahrbuch*. A number of them have been published in English, in *On the Kabbalah and Its Symbolism* and *On the Mystical Idea of the Godhead*. Eleven such studies were published in Hebrew in *Pirqe yesod be-havanat ha-qabbala u-semaleha*, Jerusalem 1975/6.

These articles go beyond *Major Trends* in their treatment of the *Zohar*'s doctrines, in two ways: the ideas of the *Zohar* are explicated at greater length, with many valuable new interpretations; and they are considered against the background of the history of ideas both preceding and following the *Zohar*'s composition. For example, in '*Shi'ur qoma* — The Mystical Shape of the Godhead' Scholem discusses the relationship between the *Zohar* and *merkava* mysticism.[20] In *Major Trends* Scholem had stressed that the kabbalists, and especially the author of the *Zohar*, were relatively uninterested in mystical contemplation of the *merkava*, whose images of the Throne of Glory and the mystical creatures and wheels surrounding it were of entities outside the Godhead; they sought, rather, to apprehend the divine Being itself by means of the symbolism of the *sefirot*. Moreover, *Major Trends* makes no comparison between the anthropomorphic portrayal of the Godhead in the *Idra rabba* of the *Zohar* and the anthropomorphic imagery in the text of the *Shi'ur qoma*, composed by the *merkava* mystics. The central theme of Scholem's article on the '*Shi'ur qoma*' is precisely such a comparison between the two mystical images.[21]

Scholem maintains that contrary to the philosophers, who either (in the view of Maimonides) regarded the vision of the *Shi'ur qoma* as a heresy to be uprooted, or attempted to obscure its nature, 'the kabbalists were not ashamed of those images, on the contrary, they saw them as repositories of the divine mysteries.'[22] However, they understood and represented the anthropomorphic divine figure as a kabbalistic system of symbols. Scholem says of the *Idrot* of the *Zohar*, where the Godhead is also described in the image — or more precisely the images — of man: 'We find a version of *Shi'ur qoma* reconceived in the spirit of the Kabbalah, in no way inferior to the ancient fragments either in boldness or, if one may phrase it thus, Gnostic presumptuousness. However, in contrast with the *Shi'ur qoma* it does not conceal its metaphysical background.'[23]

20 In *Mystical Idea of the Godhead*, pp. 15–55.
21 *Ibid.*, pp. 45–46.
22 *Ibid.*, p. 38.
23 *Ibid.*, p. 179.

This change in Scholem's views on the connection between the *Zohar* and the *Shi'ur qoma* stemmed from his later research on *merkava* mysticism, the results of which he published in *Jewish Gnosticism, Merkabah Mysticism, and Talmudic Tradition*. From a material point of view, one of his major new conclusions is formulated in the article on *Shi'ur qoma* as follows: 'The most profound of all the chapters of the *merkava* is that concerning the shape of the Deity (extant in the *Shi'ur qoma* fragments).'[24] In other words, the *merkava* mystics also contemplated the Godhead, and the anthropomorphic descriptions in the *Idrot* are to be understood as a development of the *Shi'ur qoma* vision.

In his article 'The Meaning of the Torah in Jewish Mysticism,'[25] Scholem once again examines a broad kabbalistic theme and its historical development. He enumerates three fundamental principles governing the various kabbalistic conceptions of the mystical meanings of the Torah: '(1) the principle of God's name; (2) the principle of the Torah as an organism; (3) the principle of the infinite meaning of the divine word.'[26]

Scholem's point of departure in researching the operation of these principles is an examination of rabbinic dicta cited by the kabbalists, who searched out the hidden mystical core and altered the literal meaning of these dicta to support their own novel views. Scholem used this method in studies of other subjects as well, in order to elucidate both the real and the purported relationship between the Kabbala and rabbinic literature.

The fundamental meaning of the first principle is that the Torah consists of names of God or, in a more radical version, that the entire Torah is one name of God. This idea gives the Torah a quality of divinity, like the *sefirot*, which are also conceived as a fabric woven of divine names; and it also opens the door to free-ranging mystical interpretations of Scripture. The aspect of the Torah's divinity connects the first principle with the second, according to which the Torah is a living organism with body and soul, limbs

24 *Mystical Idea of the Godhead*, p. 32.
25 In *Kabbalah and Symbolism*, pp. 36–85.
26 *Ibid.*, p. 37.

and organs; in this sense, too, the Torah mirrors the revelation and operation of the *sefirot* in the world. The second implication of the first principle, that of the freedom of mystical interpretation, connects it with the third principle, which asserts the infinite meanings of the Torah.

Scholem clarifies how these principles affected the historical development and diversity of kabbalistic conceptions, from those of Isaac the Blind and his disciples in the early thirteenth century up to the *Zohar*, and from the *Zohar* through the last throes of Sabbateanism and the beginnings of Hasidism in the eighteenth century, via the Kabbala of Safed. Sholem emphasizes the central role of the *Zohar* as a repository of ideas and as a source of innovation and continuing influence. In describing this historical development, Scholem also discusses at length the ideas of the *Ra'aya mehemana* and *Tiqqunei zohar*, the latest, anonymous parts of the *Zohar*. The implications of the principle of infinite meaning are of particular importance, for their intrinisic interest, their influence and their role in the *Zohar*'s novel interpretations. I shall attempt briefly to recapitulate some of the many aspects of Sholem's research and conclusions on this topic.

The basic conceptual structure of this principle throughout all the branches of the Kabbala from its inception is the duality of manifest and hidden, inward and outward. This duality was a well-known concept in Jewish philosophical literature prior to the emergence of the Kabbala as well. However, Jewish philosophical exegesis identified the esoteric level as rationalistic truth, to be revealed through allegorical interpretation, while the kabbalists used symbolic-mystical interpretations to uncover the kabbalistic mysteries embedded in Scripture. The author of the *Zohar* was the first kabbalist to expand this manifest-hidden duality to four levels of interpretation of the Torah, denoted by the acronym PaRDeS (*peshat, remez, derash, sod* — the literal, symbolic, homiletic and esoteric meanings). Though this type of fourfold analysis was also used by other late thirteenth-century kabbalists, the form it took in the *Zohar* was the one handed down to later generations.

Another innovation of the *Zohar* was its interpretation of the late midrashic saying, 'There are seventy faces to the Torah.'[27] According

27 *Numbers Rabba* 8:15.

to the *Zohar*, this means that every word and letter in the Torah has seventy aspects — that is, seventy esoteric meanings. This gave virtually free rein to the creative power of mystical interpretation. The kabbalists of Safed, especially Isaac Luria and his disciples, carried the principle of infinite meaning furthest. They taught that the Torah has 600,000 aspects, equivalent to the number of Israelites present at Sinai; and since they saw the soul of every Jew throughout the ages as having its root in the Exodus generation, this means that the Torah has a unique 'face' for each and every individual.

The *Ra'aya mehemana* and *Tiqqunei zohar* introduced several important new distinctions to this principle. Based on statements by the Sages that the Torah antedated the creation of the world, the anonymous author of these two tracts determined that the primordial Torah was completely spiritual, containing no prohibitions, injunctions, or practical commandments. This was the Torah of the higher world, *Tora de-'azilut*, whereas the Torah we possess, *Tora de-beri'a*, is adapted to the imperfect reality in which we live. The inferiority of the latter is evinced even more sharply in a different formulation: before the original sin there was the Torah of the Tree of Life, which was identical to the primordial, spiritual Torah; only after the Fall was it transformed into the material Torah of the Tree of Knowledge of Good and Evil, the practical Torah with all its restrictions. The advent of the Messiah will bring with it the annulment of the earthbound Torah and the restoration of its supernal, spiritual counterpart. These same ideas resurfaced among the mystics of sixteenth-century Safed, and they served as the theoretical basis for the antinomianism of the Sabbatean messianic movement.

Scholem's presentation of the doctrines of the *Zohar* in *Major Trends* was a unified whole, a 'Torah given complete,' to borrow a talmudic saying.[28] By contrast, his elucidation of the *Zohar*'s concepts in light of the historical development of particular themes was a 'Torah given scroll by scroll,'[29] over the course of several decades. The lectures in which it was presented covered almost every area of Scholem's scholarly interest — *merkava* mysticism,

28 BT *Gittin* 60a.
29 *Ibid.*

early Kabbala and its origins, the doctrine of the *Zohar*, the Kabbala of Safed, Sabbateanism and Hasidism — and they were delivered up to his very last year. There is no doubt that he planned to continue adding further storeys to the magnificent edifice he had erected in the history of ideas of Jewish mysticism. How sad the loss, and how irretrievable!

I conclude by expressing what all those who studied with Scholem or with his students, all who are engaged in the study of mysticism in general or the *Zohar* in particular, must feel. Anyone working in any area Scholem has studied draws upon and is sustained by his monumental scholarly undertaking. It has come to an end unfinished, and remains as the solid basis for the labors of generations to follow. Thus, even though he lived long and bequeathed an immense intellectual and spiritual legacy, it is still fitting in the aftermath of his passing to quote the following lines from Bialik's poem, *After I Am Dead*:

> Great, great is the pain,
> There was a man, and behold: he is no more,
> His life cut short in mid-song.

GERSHOM SCHOLEM ON PANTHEISM
IN THE KABBALA

by

J. Ben-Shlomo*

AS IN MANY other topics in Jewish mysticism, Gershom Scholem went far beyond the vague and general remarks of his predecessors to lay the enduring foundation for a discussion of pantheism in the Kabbala. He treats the subject in remarks scattered throughout his writings, and more systematically in his chapter on Moses Cordovero, the foremost sixteenth-century theologian of the pre-Lurianic Kabbala;[1] in his study of Abraham Herrera, the seventeenth-century Lurianic kabbalist who merged Lurianic Kabbala with Neoplatonic philosophy; and in the entry 'Kabbala and Pantheism' in the *Encyclopedia Judaica*.[2] These remarks, albeit scanty, paved ways for the study of pantheism, not only in the Kabbala but in mysticism in general.

Scholem also handed down some basic methodological principles to those who were fortunate enough to study with him. We learned to pay attention to seemingly irrelevant asides in the texts and to ostensibly innocent formulations that often concealed fundamental and daring statements of principle. Scholem taught us, however, not to be led astray by enthusiastically pantheistic utterances, and to apply the tools of philology even to this non-philological topic — to examine scrupulously the exact meaning of terms and concepts within their context.

Identifying pantheistic doctrines in the Kabbala is a complex task. On the one hand, almost all the kabbalists formulated their doctrines

---

* Joseph Ben-Shlomo is Professor of Philosophy and Jewish Thought at Tel Aviv University.
1 *Major Trends*, pp. 252–253.
2 Reprinted in *Kabbalah*, pp. 144–152.

in orthodox, theistic terms. On the other, what look like overtly pantheistic statements within the context of a particular kabbalistic system may, on closer analysis, shed their pantheistic coloring. The first type of difficulty is exemplified by the kabbalistic interpretation of the religious tenet of *creatio ex nihilo* (*yesh mi-'ayin*, creation from nothing). In its traditional sense, this tenet is incompatible with pantheism: God, by His absolute free will, creates an entity that is not Himself out of nothing at all, and not out of any pre-existent reality. This guarantees the absolute differentiation between God and the world, as well as the freedom of divine action. However, when *creatio ex nihilo* is interpreted symbolically, its meaning is overturned: 'Nothingness' (*'ayin*) becomes not total absence of being, but a mystical symbol of the infinite fullness of being, which, because it is beyond man's comprehension, is paradoxically called 'Nothingness.' This Nothingness is the first *sefira*, from which the First Being, that is, the second *sefira*, emerges by means of a process of emanation — and not by a spontaneous act of divine free will. If a continuous chain of causation is posited from this point, by which each level of reality, down to our material world, is emanated from that above it, this does away with the theistic understanding of the doctrine of creation. Those kabbalistic doctrines that identify the first *sefira* with the *'Ein-Sof* thus take on a markedly pantheistic coloration, for then God himself is the Nothingness from which all the worlds are formed and in which they are comprised.

This transformed meaning of *creatio ex nihilo* is an expression of the spell-binding attraction that the paradoxical symbol of Nothingness equaling infinite plenitude has for the mystic. The interpretation of 'creation from nothing' that emerges from this symbol views it as a process by which God differentiates His infinite substance into infinite aspects, creating Himself by changing from 'Natura Naturans' to 'Natura Naturata,' in Spinoza's phrase.

Scholem notes that this mystical concept appears in two forms: either God and Nothingness are understood as two different aspects of His essence, or both come together as an integral unity. Christian, Moslem, and Jewish mystics who held the first, more moderate view identified the aspect of Nothingness in God with the divine Will, by which the world was created.[3] This, however, is exactly contrary to the thrust of orthodox doctrines of creation, which seek to preserve God's unconditional and totally volitional freedom in the act of creation from absolute nothingness. If Nothingness is identified with the divine Will, then beings were not created from nothing by the divine Will. Rather, it is the revelation of the Will that constitutes creation, and there is no other creation. The pantheistic thrust of this doctrine is mitigated by separating the *'ayin*, the divine Will, from God, the infinite plenitude (*'Ein-Sof*) hidden in the depths of His divine substance, which is above being and nothingness alike. Even then, however, no act of creation takes place other than the emanation of the First Being from the divine Nothingness, the Will.

This mystical understanding of *creatio ex nihilo*, with its pantheistic overtones, appears very early on in the Kabbala, in the writings of Azriel of Gerona, a prominent member of the thirteenth-century Gerona circle of kabbalists. He states that the *'Ein-Sof* 'made Nothingness into Being' — that is, He made His own Nothingness, which is the divine Will, into His Being, which is divine Wisdom (*Hokhma*). 'Nothingness is Being and Being is Nothingness,' in the supreme unity of 'the binding of Being and Nothingness.' According to Azriel, the divine Nothingness (*'ayin*) manifests Being (*yesh*), and the divine Being encompasses Nothingness. The nature of the existence of all things in the divine Nothingness differs from the nature of their existence in the divine Being, but both are emanations of the *'Ein-Sof*, which comprises the absolute and undifferentiated unity of Being and Nothingness, and perforce of all reality. According to Scholem, this concept is reminiscent of formulations in Hegel's philosophy and in Mahayan Buddhism.[4]

In contrast to this example of how a theistic concept can take on a pantheistic coloring, Scholem demonstrates that other concepts which may seem explicitly pantheistic — even in statements by the very same Azriel — may be given an entirely theistic interpretation. Scholem claims, for instance, that the oft-repeated declaration, 'There is nothing outside of Him,' should be understood traditionally,

3 'Schöpfung,' p. 103.
4 *Ibid.*, p. 110.

58

as indicating nothing more than the absolute dependence of all beings upon the God who created them. In other words,

> Nothing could exist without a first, divine cause, and ... the latter, since it is the cause of all, includes and comprehends within itself whatever it has caused. In this respect God can be said to be present and immanent in all that He has caused, and were He to discontinue His presence all caused existence would thereby be annihilated.[5]

Scholem gives a similar interpretation to pantheistic-sounding statements by Abraham Herrera, who is regarded as one of Spinoza's sources.[6] Herrera's statement that 'The Infinite First Cause exists in and expands into all places and states which exist in actuality and *in potentia*' may sound pantheistic, but Scholem interprets it theistically, as a pronouncement that God acts in the world through a continuous chain of linked causes.[7]

In Scholem's view, even pantheistic-sounding statements by kabbalists whose entire doctrine has a pantheistic cast, like those of Abraham Azulai, author of the compendium of Cordoveran commentaries on the *Zohar*, should be understood in this way:

> Azulai states, for instance, that man is 'in communion with God,' because 'there is nothing that is separated from Him.' But the reason he adduces for this is perfectly orthodox and non-pantheistic; it is the chain of cause and effect which, in the final analysis, links God with His creation.[8]

Scholem was cautious about identifying a kabbalistic doctrine as pantheistic even according to his moderate definition, much less in a more radical sense. 'It is evident,' he declared, 'that ... not a single kabbalist school of thought ever claimed that God has no existence apart from created beings.'[9] Scholem defined pantheism in

5 *Kabbalah*, pp. 144–145.
6 *Herrera*, p. 54; Solomon Maimon was referring to Herrera's thought when he declared that 'Kabbala is nothing but expanded Spinozism.'
7 *Ibid.*, p. 62.
8 *Messianic Idea*, p. 223.
9 *Kabbalah*, p. 148.

59

the Kabbala in relation to the doctrine of the emanation of the *sefirot*: this doctrine may be called pantheistic if the *sefirot* are considered as directly emanated from God, with the Emanator's substance being immanent in all the worlds. It is not pantheistic, however, if the immanence is only of the light or power of the Emanator; and this, Scholem maintains, was indeed the position of most kabbalists:

> [They] rejected the notion that God's substance realizes itself in the world of emanation and insisted, as did most medieval neo-platonists, that God's power alone, as opposed to His substance, goes forth in the emanative process.[10]

Even those kabbalists who identified the *'Ein-Sof* with the first *sefira*, thereby making the *sefirot* a manifestation of God's substance, denied the pantheistic conclusion that was the logical outcome of their doctrine.

The same is true of kabbalistic thought on the relationship between the soul and God. Scholem pointed out that the supreme mystical experience of most kabbalists is not *Unio Mystica*, the union of the soul with God, but communion (*devequt*) with Him: 'Even in this ecstatic frame of mind, the Jewish mystic almost invariably retains a sense of the distance between the Creator and His creature.'[11] Despite some apparent exceptions which we shall discuss below, especially in Hasidism, Scholem maintains that 'such tendencies are not characteristic of Jewish mysticism.'[12] This is a point of difference between Jewish and Christian mystics:

> Whereas in Catholic mysticism 'Communion' was not the last step on the mystical way ... in Kabbalism it is the last grade of ascent to God. It is not union, because union with God is denied to man even in that mystical upsurge of the soul, according to kabbalistic theology. But it comes as near to union as a mystical interpretation of Judaism would allow.[13]

---

10 *Ibid.*, p. 145.
11 *Major Trends*, p. 123.
12 *Ibid.*
13 *Messianic Idea*, pp. 203–204.

In any event, in contrast to Christian mysticism, the question of the presence of pantheistic doctrines in Jewish mysticism turns not on this issue, but rather, as we have said, on the issue of *creatio ex nihilo*. There is a 'built-in contradiction between the doctrine of emanation and that of a paradigmatic creation, in the clash between which lay the crux of the problem of pantheism in the Kabbala.'[14] The internal logic of the doctrine of emanation leads to pantheism, and it is therefore inherently antithetical to Jewish mysticism. To this historical-phenomenological assessment Scholem added his 'unhistorical' viewpoint, as we shall see below.

Scholem's moderate evaluation of the role of pantheism in the Kabbala is in keeping with his approach to the study of Kabbala and its place within Judaism. Jewish philosophers from Saadya Gaon in the tenth century through Hermann Cohen in the nineteenth had taken the stance that Jewish monotheism must be protected from its two major enemies, myth and pantheism. As is well known, Scholem rejected this view, but undaunted by the repeated appearance of these two elements in Jewish mysticism, he attempted 'an understanding of these phenomena which yet does not lead away from monotheism.'[15] He also demonstrated that the mythic and the pantheistic, which at times seem contradictory, can appear together. For example, he showed that the mythic imagery of the *Shi'ur qoma*, the early mystical work which describes the Godhead in the form of a supernal man of colossal dimensions, could be given a pantheistic interpretation, by which 'reality in its entirety constitutes this mystical figure of the Godhead.'[16]

According to Scholem, the *Zohar* is the example *par excellence* of the blending of gnostic mythic symbolism with a strongly pantheistic coloration. Although the *Zohar* employs theistic terminology, a penetrating scrutiny brings to light its hidden pantheistic leanings, which here too, in Scholem's view, center on the topic of creation. The *Zohar*'s dual interpretation of creation, as both a process within the divine world and as cosmogony, exemplifies both its mythic

---

14 *Kabbalah*, p. 152.
15 *Major Trends*, p. 38.
16 G. Scholem, *Pirqe yesod be-havanat ha-qabbala ve-semaleha* (Hebrew transl. by J. Ben-Shlomo), Jerusalem 1976, p. 172.

character and its pantheistic tendency. Symbolically, the creation story is the description of the drama of God's revelation to Himself, via the dynamic unfolding of His powers — the *sefirot*. Even when the extra-divine World of Separation (*'alma de-peruda*) appears, its separation from the Godhead is not really unequivocal:

> All created existence has a certain kind of reality to itself in which it appears independent of these mystical worlds of unity. But in the sight of the mystic the separate outlines of things become blurred until they, too, represent nothing but the Glory of God and His Hidden Life which pulsates in everything.[17]

Moses de Leon, the pseudonymous thirteenth-century author of the *Zohar*, propounded the continuity of all the worlds more boldly in his Hebrew writings. As he states in *Sefer ha-rimmon*,

> Everything is linked with everything else down to the lowest ring on the chain, and the true essence of God is above as well as below, in the heavens and on the earth, and nothing exists outside Him. ... Meditate on these things and you will understand that God's essence is linked and connected with all worlds, and that all forms of existence are linked and connected with each other, but derived from His existence and essence.[18]

In Scholem's view, Moses de Leon also took a more definitive stand on the relationship between the soul and God in his Hebrew works, writing of the human soul as '"a part of God above" (Job 31:2), not just in a figurative sense, ... but quite literally.'[19]

Scholem saw the sixteenth-century doctrine of Moses Cordovero as the most consistent expression of the pantheistic tendency in Kabbala. His system indeed lacks the mythical quality of the *Zohar* and is characterized instead by its great speculative force. Here, too, the issue of pantheism centers on Cordovero's discussion of creation and his interpretation of the doctrine of emanation. However, the focal point is not *creatio ex nihilo* in the symbolic, mystic sense, that

17 *Major Trends*, pp. 223–224.
18 *Ibid.*, p. 223.
19 *Kabbalah*, p. 148.

is, the emergence of the second *sefira* from the first, but rather that which occurs at what he sees as the highest point of the emanation process, the transition from *'Ein-Sof* to the first *sefira*, which is the first movement from God Himself to His will to emanate. As Scholem writes in the fifth of his 'Ten Unhistorical Aphorisms on the Kabbala':

> In this sense the fundamental differentiation between the *'Ein-Sof* and the first *sefira* is connected to the problematics of pantheism. This differentiation is the focus of the problem, and Cordovero especially was fully aware that the transition from *'Ein-Sof* to the First *sefira*, the *Urakt*, is a step whose significance is infinitely greater than the sum of all the steps taken thereafter. Beginning with this act everything is in effect prescribed, for the pure turning of God to create constitutes the act of creation, even if to us it seems to have many stages and infinite processes. Within the Godhead all these are one and the same act.[20]

According to Cordovero, the world of emanation — the *sefirot* — is comprehended within the divine Will, which is itself included in the *'Ein-Sof*. Even in this highest state, where the *sefirot* are united within their source, 'they are nevertheless not truly identical with the substance of *'Ein Sof*, which apprehends them while remaining unapprehended by them.' As Scholem describes it, the *sefirot*

> approach the substance of *'Ein-Sof* asymptotically until the human intellect can no longer distinguish them. Nevertheless they retain an identity distinct from it, so that there is a kind of leap between *'Ein-Sof* and their hidden existence within it that continually approaches to infinity. ... The initial awakening of the divine Will is ... the one occasion on which true creation from nothingness takes place, for from then on the chain of causation is continuous until the material world.[21]

The paradoxical nature of this view, according to Scholem,

---

20 'Ten Unhistorical Aphorisms,' p. 212 (Biale, pp. 78–80).
21 *Kabbalah*, p. 149.

testifies to the manner in which he [Cordovero] felt torn between the theistic and the pantheistic approaches. From the human point of view all of these subsequent stages comprise a secondary reality existing separately from *'Ein-Sof* and contingent on it.

They are not identical with the substance of God, but merely 'vessels' that clothe it. However, 'from the divine point of view God comprehends all.' Nonetheless, Scholem adds:

> Even from the viewpoint of the human condition it is potentially possible to contemplatively 'undress' these garments and reveal 'the processions of the substance' (*tahalukhei ha-ezem*) which clothe themselves in them. Such a moment of revelation is the supreme happiness to which the mystic can attain in his lifetime.[22]

Scholem characterizes Cordovero's outlook as panentheistic, a modified pantheism in which all reality is comprehended within the Godhead, but is not identical with it. In Cordovero's words: 'God is all that exists, but not all that exists is God.'[23] This concept, according to Scholem, 'is entirely compatible with theism'[24] and '[leaves] room for a personalistic depiction of the Godhead.'[25]

Scholem presents Isaac Luria, in contrast to Cordovero, as 'a living example of an outspoken theistic mystic. He gave the *Zohar*

22 *Ibid.*, pp. 149–150.
23 *Ibid.*, p. 150.
24 *Herrera*, p. 61.
25 *Kabbalah*, p. 148. As Scholem's student, let me add a personal note testifying to his stature as a person and as a teacher. In my doctorate on Cordovero, written under Scholem's guidance, I proposed a thesis contrary to his regarding panentheism. Throughout the period of its composition, Scholem never once uttered a word of criticism on this subject and did not try to change my mind. Only in his assessment of my work did he remark that all of my arguments could have been used to support the opposing view. And when Scholem collected the entries on Kabbala for the *Encyclopedia Judaica*, he asked me to write the entry on Cordovero (reprinted in *Kabbalah*, pp. 401–404). He presented his own opinion in brief under the entry 'Kabbala and Pantheism,' from which the above analysis is derived (*ibid.*, pp. 149–151). I wish only to add that I have become convinced in the meantime that he was right.

a strictly theistic interpretation.'[26] It was Luria's doctrine of *zimzum* (the contraction of God within Himself to leave room for the creation of the world) that was, in the final analysis, the only impenetrable barrier to the pantheism implicit in the doctrine of emanation:

> In contrast to the doctrine of emanation, which allows only for a symbolic interpretation of creation from nothingness, the new doctrine of *zimzum* presents an entirely theistic view, for it determines ... that the primordial space from which the Godhead withdraws in the act of *zimzum* is divine Nothingness (*'ayin*).[27]

If Being (*yesh*) emerges from the divine Nothingness (*'ayin*), which is the Godhead, then how can it exist as a separate reality, independent of God? It remains, claims Scholem, 'of necessity a reality whose source is in the Godhead.'[28] Only the doctrine of *zimzum* can provide a satisfactory explanation for the existence of anything that is not divine.

To be sure, Scholem pointed to other elements in the Lurianic Kabbala that did feed into pantheistic tendencies, which came to the fore in later Kabbala. These included the ideas relating to the *reshimu*, the residue of the light of *'Ein-Sof* remaining in the primordial space created by the *zimzum*; the transformation of the *Shekhina* from a personalistic symbol into a symbol of divine immanence in the world; and the *zimzum* itself, interpreted metaphorically rather than literally, or as a naturalistic simile for 'the a priori assumption of creation.' Nonetheless, according to Scholem, 'the authentic sources of Lurianic Kabbala do not allow for such an idealistic interpretation of the *zimzum* and the primordial space.'[29] On the other hand, one of the means by which the Lurianic Kabbala guarded its strict theism was by maintaining that the world of emanation (*'olam ha-'azilut*) is not really a world in the precise meaning of the term, because it is a manifestation of the Godhead itself. The subsequent worlds of *beri'a, yezira* and *'assiya*, by contrast, were created from true nothingness by a free act of God. In other words, as opposed to the *Zohar* or

---

26 *Major Trends*, p. 262.
27 *Herrera*, p. 46.
28 'Schöpfung,' p. 115.
29 *Herrera*, p. 46.

Cordovero's thought, Lurianic doctrine considered the continuous chain of causation to start only from the world of creation (*beri'a*), and not from the world of emanation (*'azilut*). This was the argument of the eighteenth-century kabbalist Moses Hayyim Luzzatto (author of the popular ethical work *Messilat yesharim*) against any attempt to 'think that there can be any bond' — any ontological continuity — 'between what is created and the Creator.'[30]

The interpretation of the doctrine of *zimzum* became the touchstone in the clash between theistic and pantheistic tendencies in the later Kabbala, especially in Hasidism. Indeed, there was a tendency in the first period of Hasidism to interpret *zimzum* pantheistically, thus obliterating the absolute transcendence of the *'Ein-Sof* and allowing for mystical contact between the soul and God Himself. Scholem sees this tendency primarily as an expression both of the powerful mystical experiences of the first Hasidim and of the popular nature of the hasidic movement. The enthusiastic fervor of its unsophisticated adherents led them to extreme pantheistic formulations, in contradistinction to the classical Kabbala, 'which reflected something of the complicated ambiguity of the subject.'[31] Here, too, Scholem cautions against making too much of pantheistic-sounding statements. The founder of the hasidic movement, the Baal Shem Tov, may have made frequent use of such traditional verses and phrases as 'Everything is full of His glory,' 'there is no place void of Him,' or 'Thou keepest them all alive,' but his doctrine was at most panentheistic.[32] To those who saw in it something resembling the pantheistic tendencies of Spinoza, Scholem replied:

> I think that the numerous writers who have compared the Baal Shem's teaching to that of Spinoza have considerably overshot the mark. I for one, am unable to find any teachings reminiscent of Spinoza in the Baal Shem's doctrinal sayings.[33]

---

30 *Kabbalah*, p. 151.
31 *Major Trends*, p. 347.
32 *Messianic Idea*, p. 223.
33 *Ibid.*, p. 224.

To be sure, there are acosmic tendencies in early Hasidism: the world of phenomena is 'denied real existence, reality is seen rather as a sort of "veil of Maya".' But again, Scholem stresses,

> The ideational content of the formula is, almost in every case, limited to a much less radical interpretation, by reading into it either the doctrine of divine immanence or that of the annihilation of reality before the contemplative mind. For if one looks closely into the context of such passages, all that remains of the high-flown formulas is always the omnipresence of the divine influxus, *shefa*, and *hiyut*, the vitalizing power, instead of that of the divine substance.[34]

Scholem was careful not to read pantheistic significance even into overtly pantheistic formulations, like the declaration of the hasidic master Pinhas of Koretz that 'If a man fulfills the commandments of the Torah ... then he lifts up the whole universe to its "root" above, *for the world is really God Himself.*'[35] Scholem demonstrates that this statement refers to the mystical experience in which the mystic rises, together with all created beings, to their root in the Naught (*'ayin*). At this point 'they lose their identity as creatures, because all that can be beheld there is God alone.'[36] Scholem emphasizes, however, that

> we should not forget that, to reach that state, creation as creation must be 'annihilated,' which implies that creation, in its own right, is not what pantheism would declare it to be, namely a mere mode of Infinity.[37]

Such a conception, according to Scholem, was at most panentheistic.

In the thinking of Azriel of Gerona or Cordovero, the issue of pantheism arose out of metaphysical speculation on the relationship between God and the world. Scholem's remarks on the subject indicate that this was far less true of Hasidism (though he dealt very little

34 *Ibid.*
35 *Ibid.*, p. 225.
36 *Ibid.*
37 *Ibid.*

with Habad Hasidism and later hasidic doctrines). The mysticism of the early Hasidim focused mainly on the relationship between God and man, and it was this preoccupation that gave a pantheistic tone to their statements about the world. The acosmic conception expresses 'a degree of abandonment to emotionalism that has no precedent.'[38] This depth of feeling lay at the heart of the development by the Maggid of Mezritch, successor of the Baal Shem Tov, of the idea that all beings return to the divine Nothingness (*'ayin*) through the process of *devequt*, which transforms the Ego (*'ani*) into Nothingness (*'ayin*). Scholem notes that this line of thought may be traced from the first Hasidim back to the early neoplatonist kabbalistic thought of Azriel, who states in his 'Principles on the Secret of Prayer' that 'one who prays returns things to their Nothingness.'[39] But the 'return of things to their Nothingness' does not obliterate the differentiation between Creator and creation; by means of cleaving to the Nothingness (*'ayin*), the created being draws the divine influxus (*shefa*) necessary for his existence. This idea, declares Scholem, is far indeed from the pantheistic deification that occasionally appears in Christian mysticism and that characterizes the mystical doctrines of the Far East.

Nonetheless, 'the Maggid of Mezritch went far on the way of what must be described as mystical intoxication';[40] his interpretation of *devequt* is the most radical of early Hasidism. The Maggid's explanation of the verse 'Make thee two trumpets of silver' (Numbers 10:2) is a case in point. He presents a correlative model of man and God: man without God is not truly man, and only when man and God are in true union does man realize his full nature. This is achieved by the constant striving and longing for union with God, in which man casts off all material elements until he is 'one with God.' In other words, 'man finds himself by losing himself in God, and by giving up his identity, he discovers it on a higher plane.'[41] According to the Maggid, then, *devequt* is not only communion with God but

---

38 *Ibid.*, p. 214.
39 'Schöpfung,' p. 119.
40 *Messianic Idea*, p. 226.
41 *Ibid.*, p. 227.

union (*ahdut*) with Him. Even in the face of this daring conception, however, Scholem warns us

> not to lose ourselves in his terminology, which is radical indeed, but to consider the context of his thought. ... This union is, in fact, not at all the pantheistic obliteration of the self within the divine mind which he likes to call the Naught, but pierces through this state on to the rediscovery of man's spiritual identity. ... This, then, is the deepest meaning of *devequt* of which Hasidism knows, and the radical terms should not blind us to the eminently Jewish and personalistic conception of man which they still cover. After having gone through *devequt* and union, man is still man — nay, he has, in truth only then started to be man, and it is only logical that only then will he be called upon to fulfill his destiny in the society of men.[42]

Scholem's greatness lay in his ability to describe the historical material objectively, in his penetrating assessment of its phenomenology, and in his intellectual honesty, which remained untinged by personal biases. However, Scholem did also write ten 'Unhistorical Aphorisms' on the Kabbala, as well as an essay on Jewish theology, and from these we can garner something of his personal views concerning pantheism in Judaism.

In the seventh of those unhistorical aphorisms, Scholem writes:

> The doctrine of emanation, like many abortive forms of mysticism, is perhaps the true catastrophe of Kabbala. The penetrating vision of the kabbalists centered on the structures of being. Nothing is more detrimental than confusing the relationship between these structures and the doctrine of emanation.[43]

We have seen that, according to Scholem, the internal logic of the doctrine of emanation leads to the negation of the principle of creation — in other words, to pantheism, especially when the first *sefira*, the divine Nothingness or *'ayin*, is identified with the *'Ein-Sof*. The kabbalists who rejected this identification sensed its

---

42 *Ibid.*, pp. 226–227.
43 'Ten Unhistorical Aphorisms,' p. 214 (Biale, pp. 85–86).

fundamental flaw: it lacked the dialectical element inherent in the idea of creation. Scholem writes:

> This absence of dialectic is what makes this assertion unable to withstand pantheism; without transcendence Nothingness extends down to Somethingness ... creation from Nothingness is but a mark of the essential unity of all things with God ... the mystic who treats his experiences undialectically must end up in pantheism.[44]

Scholem emphasizes that the monotheistic idea of creation is of necessity dialectic, for it posits a being separate from God while at the same time conceiving of God as an infinite whole. But if God's infinity is taken seriously, how can there be an ontological place for any reality other than Him? This was Spinoza's clinching argument against any form of monotheism that, inconsistently, did not turn into pantheistic monism. Spinoza's reasoning can be countered only by positing a paradoxical process like that of *zimzum* preceding any process of emanation. Even if, after the act of *zimzum*, the *'Ein-Sof* then emanates its light into the primordial space that is the Naught (*'ayin*), God's contraction of His plenitude must recur in every stage of emanation — and in the formation of all reality. If not for this, anything non-divine would cease to exist, and only God would remain. So

> there is a profound dialectic in all reality which comes into being after the *zimzum*; all being contains the Nothingness which is created by the *zimzum*.[45]

Scholem ultimately discerns this sense of the dialectic nature of the concept of creation even in the earliest kabbalistic doctrines concerning the relationship between *'Ein-Sof* and the first *sefira*. As he says in that fifth aphorism:

> For what does the differentiation between these ultimately mean? Precisely this: that the essential plenitude of the hidden God, which remains transcendent with respect to all knowledge (even

44 *Ibid.*, pp. 212–213 (*ibid.*, p. 80).
45 'Schöpfung,' p. 117.

intuitive knowledge), becomes Nothingness ... which is above all the pure turning towards creation.[46]

This Nothingness of God, to be distinguished from God's substance, is what guarantees the status of the world as creation, in the non-pantheistic sense.

Only the doctrine of *zimzum* offers an affirmative and meaningful answer to the other crucial question posed by all theistic doctrines of creation — the question of God's freedom. In Scholem's view, the doctrine of *zimzum* is the quintessential expression of God's absolute freedom in the act of creation:

> This is the essential content of such freedom: i.e., the freedom to limit — even if only at one point — the infinite perfection and plenitude of His substance.[47]

Scholem stated his anti-pantheistic position clearly and simply in an essay on Jewish theology:

> No Jewish theology whatever can renounce the doctrine that the world is a creation — as a one-time event or as a continual always self-renewing process. ... The Jewish faith in God as Creator will maintain its place, beyond all images and myths.[48]

For Scholem, that faith was the basis for negating any kind of naturalism that would render the world devoid of significance:

> Any living Judaism, no matter what its concept of God, will have to oppose pure naturalism with a definite no. It will have to insist that the currently so widespread notion of a world that develops out of itself and even is capable of independently producing the phenomenon of meaning — altogether the least comprehensible of all phenomena — can, to be sure, be maintained, but not seriously held. ... It will never be possible to prove the assumption that the world has a meaning by extrapolating from limited

---

46 'Ten Unhistorical Aphorisms,' p. 212 (Biale, p. 79).
47 'Schöpfung,' p. 117.
48 *Jews and Judaism*, pp. 277–278.

71

contexts of meaning, yet it is the basic conviction underlying faith in creation.[49]

This lesson about the significance of the world *qua* creation is a legacy of as great importance as the magisterial scholarship that Scholem has bequeathed to us and to generations to come.

[49] *Ibid.*

GERSHOM SCHOLEM AND JEWISH MESSIANISM

by

Joseph Dan[*]

I

THE ROLE of Gershom Scholem's studies in transforming the attitude of Jewish historians to the messianic element in Judaism is comparable to the importance of his achievements in changing scholarly conceptions about Jewish mysticism. Once viewed as an embarrassing, marginal aberration of Jewish culture, messianism is now regarded as one of the most potent elements shaping Jewish history. The following pages will present the highlights of Scholem's research in this area. Such a survey must, however, begin with two critical negative points of departure. Scholem demonstrated both that Jewish messianism and Jewish mysticism are not inherently or consistently interrelated, and that messianic movements are not necessarily linked to catastrophes in Jewish history. These conclusions form the first stage of Scholem's revolutionary analysis of Jewish messianism.

One of the singular characteristics of Scholem's scholarship was his strict adherence to a clearly defined program of research. His 1925 letter to Bialik,[1] in which he presented his plans for the study of Jewish mysticism, faithfully predicts the course of his work from 1925 until his death in 1982, a span of nearly sixty years. All of Scholem's scholarly articles during his long career were devoted to various figures, books, events and themes in the history of Jewish mysticism — except for his detailed study, 'Towards an

---

[*] Joseph Dan is Gershom Scholem Professor of Kabbalah at The Hebrew University of Jerusalem.
1 *Devarim be-go*, pp. 59–63.

Understanding of the Messianic Idea in Judaism.'[2] This essay, which surveys the history of the messianic idea from biblical times to the twelfth century, makes almost no mention of Jewish mysticism. This, despite the fact that the periods discussed are those of the development of ancient Jewish mysticism, of the *Hekhalot* and *Merkava* literature, and of the beginnings of Jewish mysticism and Kabbala in Europe. The reason for this 'omission' is given in Scholem's other important study of Jewish messianism, 'The Messianic Idea in Kabbalism.'[3] The first half of this essay explains why the early Kabbala did not deal with messianism and why, for so many centuries, Jewish mystics displayed no special interest in the messianic idea. The second half details the dramatic change that occurred in the relationship between mysticism and messianism during the fifteenth and sixteenth centuries.

According to Scholem, these two central elements in Judaism existed side by side for centuries, even millennia, without interacting. The link between messianism and various schools of Jewish mysticism was forged in the late medieval and early modern periods, profoundly affecting the course of Jewish history and culture. However, this relatively late development was not a necessary consequence of the intrinsic characteristics of either Jewish messianism or Jewish mysticism, as many scholars believed. Scholem gives two reasons for the tendency to view these ideas as aspects of a single phenomenon. The first is that the intense messianic expectations of the period from the fifteenth through the nineteenth centuries really were inspired, at least partially, by mystical and primarily kabbalistic symbolism. The second is the bias of many nineteenth-century (and some twentieth-century) Jewish scholars, who regarded both messianism and mysticism as superstitions, and so took them as parts of the same embarrassing phenomenon. By treating each as an individual historical and cultural force, and by analyzing their separate historical development, Scholem showed that each is an independent element of Jewish spiritual life.

2 In *Messianic Idea*, pp. 1–36.
3 *Ibid.*, pp. 37–48.

Scholem found no messianic element in ancient Jewish mysticism, which flourished between the second and seventh centuries C.E.[4] The mystical schools of the *yorde merkava* ('descenders to the chariot,' based on the vision in chapter 1 of Ezekiel) were interested in the structure of the divine world, and concentrated their efforts on transporting their own souls to the celestial palaces in order to face the magnificent King of Kings, sitting on the Throne of Glory, and to join in the praises of the ministering angels.[5] There was no place in this framework for a communal or national effort to hasten the redemption. Mystics therefore seem to have had no part in the sustained and intense Jewish messianic activity that took place throughout late antiquity,[6] while messianism incorporated no mystical symbols or speculations.

Nor was the messianic idea an important feature of the new schools of Jewish mysticism that began to develop in medieval Europe in the twelfth century. Not that Jewish mystics did not believe in the redemption and the advent of the messiah; this belief simply did not pertain to their mystical world. The *Hasidei Ashqenaz* — the leaders of the Jewish mystical-pietistic movements in Germany in the twelfth and thirteenth centuries — did attempt to determine the date of the future redemption,[7] but neither their esoteric speculations

4 See *Major Trends*, pp. 40–78; and *Jewish Gnosticism*. Scholem discusses this subject further in his synoptic studies, 'Shekhinah: The Feminine Element in Divinity' and 'Shi'ur Komah: The Mystical Shape of the Godhead,' both in *Mystical Idea of the Godhead*.
It has since come to light that messianic elements do appear in this ancient mystical literature. *Hekhalot rabbati* contains an apocalypse describing the destruction of Rome, interwoven with the story of the martyrdom of the ten sages, and it also includes a reference to God awaiting the 'descenders to the chariot' in a messianic context. One of the most important Hebrew apocalyptical treatises, *Sefer Zerubavel*, is related to the *Hekhalot* literature. See J. Dan, *Ancient Jewish Mysticism*, Tel Aviv 1989, pp. 134–143.
5 See *Major Trends*, pp. 71–72.
6 An exception is perhaps Rabbi Akiva, who is described in the talmudic traditions both as a mystic (Tosefta Hagiga 11,4) and as a supporter of the messianically inspired Bar Kokhba revolt. However, these traditions never connect the messianic and the mystical aspects of Rabbi Akiva's personality.
7 *Major Trends*, pp. 87–89. Much more material on this is found in the esoteric works of the *Hasidei Ashqenaz*, but for them *kiddush ha-shem* (martyrdom) was the ultimate religious achievement.

nor their ethical program had messianic features. The same is true of the first hundred years of the development of the Kabbala, from the late twelfth to the late thirteenth century. No messianic elements can be found in the *Bahir*, the earliest known kabbalistic work, or in the kabbalistic schools of Provence and Gerona in the thirteenth century. The absence of a messianic element in early Kabbala is explained by its preoccupation with the 'Secret of Creation' (*ma'ase bereshit*). Its energies were directed to describing, via mystical symbols, the descent of divine light from the hidden, supreme Godhead, stage by stage, to the created world. This process of emanation brought forth the ten *sefirot* and thence the celestial and earthly creatures; it was, as it were, a ladder leading away from the supreme unity of the Godhead to the multiplicity of created beings. The same ladder, in the mystical view, could be used as a means to ascend back into the realm of supernal unity, a process that meant facing away from the created world to seek the pure spirituality of pre-creation times. The intent of the mystics was thus to ignore the reality around them, escaping from it deep into the remote past — towards God, but also away from both history and the future. Mystical perfection was to be sought in the secret of creation rather than in the future messianic redemption. The mystics were thus not interested in historical activity, and they turned their backs on the messianic endeavor. The beginning and early development of the Kabbala is completely free of messianic elements, and Scholem's *magnum opus* on this crucial chapter in the history of Jewish mysticism hardly mentions this theme.[8]

However, Scholem did point out, in detail, one of the most important potentially messianic elements that developed in the early Kabbala, the concept of the *shemittot* or cosmic cycles. According to this doctrine, which was known already in the Gerona circle of kabbalists in the first half of the thirteenth century, the world exists for a certain allotted time, usually six millennia. The completion of that time is followed by redemption, the destruction of the world and the creation of a new one. Each such world has its own Torah, different in character from those of the other epochs. Each epoch,

---

8 G. Scholem, *Origins of the Kabbalah*, ed. R.J. Zvi Werblowsky, Princeton–Philadelphia 1987; see also *Messianic Idea*, pp. 38–39.

moreover, is identified with one of the *sefirot*, which dominates the Torah of that epoch. The present world, obviously, is dominated by *din*, justice, law and commandment. The next world will be dominated by divine mercy, and many of the strictures of the present Torah will be replaced by expressions of unlimited divine love. In a brilliant analogy, Scholem pointed out the affinity of this concept with the teachings of Joachim of Fiore (1145–1202), who spoke of three ages of the universe, corresponding to three testaments, each dominated by an element of the Christian trinity. The Old Testament represents the Father, the New Testament (i.e., the present age) the Son, and both will eventually be superseded by the complete, eternal testament of the Holy Spirit. Some of Joachim's disciples regarded the writings of their master as the *Testamentum Aeternum* of the third age, setting off a 'messianic' turmoil in the Christian world. Analyzing the relationship between these Christian and Jewish systems, Scholem emphasized that the former predicts a revolutionary change within history, while the Jewish doctrine of the *shemittot* delays this upheaval to the time after the creation of a new world, and so cannot be regarded as acutely messianic. Its inherent messianic potential was activated, however, in the seventeenth century, when Sabbatean theologians set it in the context of the history of this world.

Another messianic element in the early Kabbala is found in treatises written by Rabbi Isaak ha-Cohen of Castile in the second half of the thirteenth century. Rabbi Isaak gave a radical turn to the concept of evil in the Kabbala, postulating a system of evil divine emanations, parallel (on the left side) to the good ones, and creating a detailed myth describing the victory of the messiah over these evil powers. In the history of Jewish mysticism, messianism is often associated with an intensification of the dualistic conception of evil. The myth of the evil powers tends to be closely related to the development of apocalyptic messianism.[9] Messianism plays a much larger role in the *Zohar* than in earlier Kabbala. Nonetheless, according

---

9 See J. Dan, 'The Emergence of Messianic Mythology in Thirteenth-Century Kabbalah in Spain,' in *Occident and Orient — A Tribute to the Memory of A. Scheiber*, Budapest–Leiden 1988, pp. 57–68.

to Scholem, 'Kabbalah and Messianism are not yet dovetailed into a genuinely organic whole' in this major work.[10] Although recent studies indicate that the messianic element was more central to the *Zohar* than previously believed,[11] possibly reflecting the influence of some of its sources,[12] it is nonetheless true that the Kabbala did not inspire a Jewish messianic movement during the thirteenth and fourteenth centuries. This situation changed dramatically in the fifteenth century, a change whose process Scholem studied in detail. His findings made it impossible to regard mysticism and messianism as integrally related religious phenomena in Judaism. Rather, the profoundly interesting question is why and how these two separate elements became fused in the fifteenth through nineteenth centuries.

II

As mentioned above, the nineteenth-century view equating mysticism and messianism was probably the product of its proponents' conception of Judaism as a purely rationalistic monotheism, in relation to which these phenomena were marginal and 'inappropriate.' The same apologetic motivation apparently explains the tendency of these historians to portray Jewish messianism as an outgrowth of the frequent persecutions and catastrophes that befell the Jewish people in the Middle Ages and modern times. Their message was: 'When left alone, Jews are rational and not led astray by messianic nonsense. They cling to this absurd notion only when they face unendurable hardships.' Jewish historiography of the nineteenth century and part of the twentieth presented persecutions and messianic movements almost as aspects of a single phenomenon.

Scholem met the full force of this apologetic prejudice in his study of the beginnings of the Sabbatean movement in the seventeenth

10 *Messianic Idea*, p. 39.
11 See the detailed study by Y. Liebes, 'The Messiah of the Zohar: On R. Simon bar Yohai as a Messianic Figure,' in idem, *Studies in the Zohar*, Albany, N.Y., 1993, pp. 1–84.
12 On messianism in the second half of the thirteenth century and the sources of Zoharic messianism, see J. Dan, 'The Beginnings of Messianic Myth in Thirteenth-Century Kabbala' (in Hebrew), in Zvi Baras (ed.), *Messianism and Eschatology — A Collection of Essays*, Jerusalem 1983, pp. 239–252.

century. Previous Jewish historians had posited that the rapid spread of belief in Sabbetai Zevi as the messiah and Nathan of Gaza as his prophet in 1665–1666 was a response to the terrible massacres of Jews in Poland and the Ukraine during the 1648–1649 Chmelnitzki revolt. They explained the fifteen-year gap between the persecutions in Eastern Europe and the appearance of Sabbateanism in Turkey by theorizing that Sabbateanism first developed in secret, forming esoteric circles of believers who became active publicly only in 1665. But Scholem, who dedicated many years to collecting and analyzing every piece of evidence that could shed some light on the development of Sabbateanism, failed to find even the smallest indication of any connection between the persecutions in Poland and Sabbetai Zevi's ideology and messianic claims. Similarly, no evidence was found to support the theory of the existence of circles of Sabbatean believers prior to the appearance of Nathan of Gaza in 1665. Scholem concluded that Sabbateanism developed independently of any direct influence by the Chmelnitzki catastrophe, an assertion reinforced by the intensive studies of other scholars over the past few decades.

The attempt to link messianism with persecutions was based on a refusal to regard messianism as an independent spiritual and cultural force within the framework of Jewish religion. Scholem showed that messianism is a constant component of Jewish belief, even though, historically, it may for long periods take the form of a subdued undercurrent. It is expressed differently in each period and by each cultural and ideological group, but its presence must always be taken into account. A study of the history of Jewish messianism should therefore encompass the complexity of its expressions and the varied motivations that bring it to the fore. Scholem described some of the basic characteristics of Jewish messianism in his phenomenological study, 'The Messianic Idea in Judaism.'[13]

III

Scholem viewed messianism as an integral part of the Jewish conception of history. An understanding of the development of the

---

13 See above, note 2.

messianic idea entails a comprehension of Judaism's view of its own history, and of social and even cosmic history. The major difference between Judaism and Christianity in this respect is that Christianity spiritualizes the concept of messianic redemption, removing it from the historical to the inner, spiritual realm, whereas Judaism has always insisted that messianic redemption is a historical occurrence.[14] Judaism could not accept the denigration of the national, social and cosmic dimensions of redemption, its presentation as an event played out in the individual soul. The various chiliastic movements within Christianity, often decried as heretical and inimical to Christian orthodoxy, are in fact, phenomenologically speaking, 'Judaizing' heresies, expressing a desire to return to the original Jewish conception of messianism.[15]

Scholem concentrated on the rabbinic period in presenting his typology of Jewish conceptions of messianism, although he found this typology applicable to later periods as well. He distinguished three attitudes towards the messianic element: conservative, restorative and utopian.[16] The conservative attitude, represented mainly by the world of *halakha*, is present-oriented, setting the messianic era beyond the realm of human pursuit. It is the latter two attitudes that are dominant in messianic movements: restorative desires for the revival of Jewish independence and the rebuilding of the Temple, and utopian aspirations for a revolutionary and miraculous state of existence in the messianic future.

Jewish attitudes towards history fit neatly into the same typology: there is a conservative tendency to work within the present and try to improve it; a restorative tendency seeking the re-establishment of an ideal past; and a utopian tendency aspiring to a radically different future. In the worldview of every historical Jewish group, sect and ideological movement, attitudes towards messianism and towards history have been almost identical. Scholem's understanding

---

14 Spiritualization of the messianic element appears in some statements by rebbes of the modern hasidic movement in the late eighteenth and early nineteenth centuries. See R. Shatz, *Quietistic Elements in Eighteenth-Century Hasidic Thought* (in Hebrew), Jerusalem 1968, pp. 168–177.

15 *Messianic Idea*, p. 16.

16 'The Messianic Idea in Judaism,' in *Messianic Idea*, pp. 3–4.

of the intimate connection between the two is manifest in the very structure of his analysis. He evinced no interest in phenomenological analyses of the origins of Jewish messianism, or of the reasons for its integrality to Judaism (and Christianity). He saw messianism as part and parcel of Jewish attitudes towards national and cosmic history, at once their cause and their result. His studies focused, rather, on the development of the messianic idea throughout history, and on assessing the impact of messianic conceptions upon how Jews confronted present, past and future.

Scholem emphasized two widely prevalent characteristics of Jewish messianism, the catastrophic and the miraculous or transcendent elements. Apocalyptics, mystical and otherwise, saw the emergence of the redeemed 'next world' as requiring the destruction of the present one. The abundant apocalyptic literature of the Second Temple period detailed the cosmic, social and national catastrophes that were expected to accompany messianic redemption. This literary genre continued to develop during the talmudic period, and several of its motifs found their way into midrashic texts and into the *Hekhalot* and *Merkava* texts of the early Jewish mystics. Throughout medieval and early modern times, up to and including the Sabbatean movement of the seventeenth and eighteenth centuries, Jews continued to write apocalyptic texts. These present a vision of the complete history of the world, encompassing past and present as well as utopian visions of the future.

This apocalyptic-utopian version of messianism, with its emphasis on the catastrophic nature of the redemptive process, was staunchly opposed by Jewish rationalists, especially Maimonides, the foremost medieval Jewish halakhic scholar and philosopher. Scholem dedicated the second half of his essay on the messianic idea to a detailed analysis of Maimonides' description of the messianic era in the concluding chapter of the *Mishne Tora*. Maimonides differed from the apocalyptic-utopian Jewish visionaries first and foremost in his insistence on the uninterrupted continuity of history. Redemption, according to Maimonides, will not put an end to history. The laws of nature and society will not be abrogated; the messianic era will bring solutions to Judaism's social and national problems, but will not fundamentally transform the character of

81

human existence in the physical world. Even more important is the insistence of Maimonides that messianic redemption will bring no change in the nature of religious worship; it will alter neither the ritual and ethical commandments nor the spiritual and intellectual adherence to God that is the most important part of religion for the rationalists. The messiah's advent will only signal more favorable physical circumstances for these activities, so that the individual will be able to seek his God in relative tranquility.

An element common to both the utopian-apocalyptic writers and their rationalist opponents is their conception of biblical texts relating to the messianic era as riddles to be solved, enigmatic statements to be interpreted. Both groups relied on biblical exegesis to substantiate their preconceived notions. According to Scholem, the apocalyptic writers went even further; they saw the whole field of messianic speculation as esoteric and intentionally concealed from the public, so that information about it could be gained only through veiled hints and symbolic allusions.

The second prevalent characteristic of Jewish messianism is the transcendent, miraculous nature of the envisioned redemption. Scholem repeatedly emphasized that most ancient and medieval Jewish descriptions of the messianic era regard the advent of the redemptive process as the exclusive prerogative of God, independent of human behavior or religious achievement. Neither Jewish apocalyptic literature nor the talmudic texts dealing with the subject put forward any set of conditions that must be fulfilled prior to the appearance of the messiah; and rabbinic promises connecting it with the performance of specific commandments should not, observes Scholem, be regarded as theological pronouncements. Ancient and most of medieval Judaism viewed the redemption not as an earthly, historical process, but as the intrusion of an external, transcendent force into history, bringing about its end.

IV

A dramatic change in Jewish attitudes towards messianism occurred in the second half of the fifteenth century, culminating in the Lurianic Kabbala of the late sixteenth century and the Sabbatean movement of the seventeenth and eighteenth centuries. Developing themes found in earlier Kabbala from the second half of the thirteenth century onwards, Jewish mystics gradually came to see messianic redemption as a historical process, whose unfolding depends on human religious activity. Many of Scholem's best-known studies are dedicated to an analysis of this ideological revolution and its consequences, as expressed in the messianic works of the expulsion period, in the Lurianic myth of the process of creation and of cosmic history, in the theology of the Sabbatean movement, and in the subsequent hasidic neutralization of the messianic element. It is in this period that Jewish messianism fused with Jewish history and became one of the most powerful forces shaping the attitudes of Jews towards themselves and the surrounding world in late medieval and early modern times.

The most important factor in this transformation was the new sense of exile that pervaded Jewish consciousness as a consequence of the expulsion of the Jews from Spain in 1492, which destroyed the largest and most influential Jewish center in medieval Europe. Earlier kabbalistic ideas about the impact of human effort upon developments within the Godhead, by means of religious and mystical worship, acquired new force and significance. This ability to influence the divine processes gave the Jew the power to hasten redemption. The whole body of the commandments, the entire realm of ethical behavior, became tools given by God to humankind in order to enable it to participate in and even to dominate the divine processes and bring about the messianic era.

This revolution, most clearly expressed in Lurianic Kabbala, to some extent internalized the messianic phenomenon, locating the center of the redemptive process within the heart of the Jewish individual. Every human thought and deed was perceived as having an impact, positive or negative, on a mystical process that determines the status of the divine powers. Although this new attitude had something in common with the spiritualization of messianism in early Christianity, there was also a cardinal difference: while in Christianity both the process of redemption and its results occur within the soul of the devout individual, in Lurianic Kabbala the result of the process is to redeem the divine powers, the cosmos as a whole and the course of history.

One element was missing in Jewish messianism from the talmudic period up to the seventeenth century: the personal messiah, the individual who brings forth the redemption. In the apocalyptic literature and after, this figure remained vague and secondary in Jewish discussions of the messianic redemption. Unlike Christian messianism, which was bound up with the figure of Jesus, or the Shiite vision of redemption, centering on the hidden *imam*, Jewish messianism did not look to a personal figure shaping and dominating the messianic drama. The Sabbatean movement changed all that: the theology of Nathan of Gaza placed an individual, Sabbetai Zevi, at the heart of the messianic process. He was the divine messenger and himself a divine power. His mission was to carry out those parts of the messianic process that ordinary human beings, aided only by the religious and ethical commandments, could not effect alone. The transcendent element of Jewish messianism thus re-emerged in Sabbatean theology, in that it spoke of a divine messenger intervening in the historical process and bringing it to an end; however, the agent of intervention took a new form, that of a messiah who was already present and involved in the historical process.

Nearly two hundred years of Jewish mystical thought, from the mid-seventeenth century to the mid-nineteenth, are characterized by the struggle between the conservative forces within Judaism and these new, historical-activistic ideas originating in the thought of Isaac Luria and Nathan of Gaza. Primarily mystically motivated and kabbalistically inspired, the conservative forces sought to reinstate messianic redemption as a transcendent, miraculous event. They gained the upper hand in the hasidic movement, neutralizing the messianic upheaval[17] and returning, in a new way, to the sharp face-off between history and redemption.[18]

---

17 This conclusion by Scholem set off a bitter controversy between him and Isaiah Tishby. At the Fourth World Congress of Jewish Studies, held in Jerusalem in 1965, Tishby delivered a lecture on the messianic element in Hasidism, published in *Zion*, XXXII (1967), pp. 1–45. Scholem responded immediately with a forceful rebuttal, which was published in the *Journal of Jewish Studies*, XX (1969), pp. 20–55. On this dispute see J. Dan, 'The Scholarly Achievements of the Late Isaiah Tishby,' in *Jewish Studies*, XXXII (1992), pp. 49–60 (in Hebrew).

18 To the best of my knowledge, Scholem did not deal with the emergence

V

Scholem concluded his major essay on Jewish messianism with an observation and a question. He observed that messianism prevents any human accomplishment in the pre-messianic era from being final. History awaits its culmination, which will come about when a transcendent force intervenes arbitrarily to transform the nature of existence. Until then, everything done by human beings is provisional and of secondary significance. Scholem described a dialectic tension between existence and messianism, the latter being fundamentally 'anti-existential.' He also observed that Judaism paid a heavy price when it attempted to break out of this dilemma and bring messianism into the plane of history, as in the Sabbatean heresy. His question was: How does the Jewish determination to participate in history in modern times, to create ultimate historical facts like the Jewish state, relate to its past experience and to the internal dynamics that shaped the various messianic attitudes?

Scholem clearly distinguished between Zionism and messianism even in his formulation of the question, presenting them as alternatives rather than as aspects of a single phenomenon. Zionism is an 'existential,' political movement, rebelling against the then-regnant view that historical activity in an unredeemed world is futile. It claims that historical achievements can be brought about without transcendent intervention. Zionism, according to this conception, is a complete departure from all the conflicting views and attitudes of Jewish messianism. It rebels against the demand to wait for divine redemption and refuses to view itself as the culmination of a redemptive process. Unlike Sabbateanism, it does not declare that Jewish entry into history is now possible because the messiah has

---

of messianism in contemporary Hasidism, a development most evident in the Habad sect but also present in other prominent hasidic groups. This contemporary trend does not necessarily indicate the presence of a suppressed messianic current in earlier hasidic thought. Nevertheless, the dialectical development among the various hasidic schools of a tendency to neutralize the messianic element, on the one hand, and of acute messianic endeavor, on the other, has yet to be studied.

Joseph Dan

come. Rather, it claims that Jewish participation in history is now
necessary and possible despite the fact that the messiah has not
come. Its endeavors are uninfluenced by the messiah's absence or
presence. Jewish participation in history is a fact as well as an urgent
necessity.

When he wrote this essay on the messianic idea, Scholem was
unsure if Judaism's new enterprise would succeed, and whether it
would escape the heavy price paid in previous centuries for messianic
endeavors. A great deal has happened since Scholem made these
remarks; the problem of the relationship between Zionism and
messianism has assumed new dimensions and a greater urgency.
Throughout his life, Scholem consistently opposed any attempt to
incorporate transcendent elements into Zionist thought, and especially to 'promise' the success of Zionism on the basis of religious,
messianic, or mystical calculations. If the Jewish people has entered
the world's historical arena by creating the Zionist movement, it must
completely accept the 'existential,' non-messianic laws governing
this arena. We know well the high price paid by the Jewish people
when it tried to 'hasten the end' and achieve messianic goals, from
the time of Bar Kokhba to that of Sabbetai Zevi. If the Jewish national
endeavor has now achieved its freedom from the transcendent, it is
challenged by historical rather than apocalyptical and eschatological
obstacles. What price will this new freedom entail? Only future
events can tell.[19]

---

19 These lines are being written immediately after the signing of the accords
between the government of Israel and the Palestine Liberation Organization
in Washington, D.C., on 13 September 1993. Scholem would have applauded
this event as the ultimate negation of messianic politics and the whole-
hearted acceptance of the historical element in Zionism.

GERSHOM SCHOLEM'S INTERPRETATION OF HASIDISM AS AN EXPRESSION OF HIS IDEALISM

by

Rivka Schatz

I

GERSHOM SCHOLEM described eighteenth-century Hasidism as 'practical mysticism at its highest.'[1] It was 'practical' because, in his view, the best of hasidic thought is not concerned with speculative mystical theory, as was the classical Kabbala; and it was 'at its highest,' even though he refused to screen out the folk-magical elements and extravagant flights of mysticism that were not always to the taste of other scholars. He was both just and generous to Hasidism. The broad scope of his vision enabled Scholem to produce a phenomenological picture of Hasidism that highlighted the contours of its ideas and their *Sitz im Leben* in society. Apart from Eliezer Zweifel's interesting attempt in the last century to understand the motivations behind the hasidic movement, this had hardly been done, despite the volumes written on the history of Hasidism. Scholem proved generous in his refusal to either 'improve' or deprecate those aspects of Hasidism that he found incompatible with his own value system.

Contemporary scholarship of Hasidism has certainly not been free of bias. Samuel Horodezky, Martin Buber and Scholem all sought to forge new paths in this area, and each set forth his own opinions both from the outset and *ex post facto*. The same is true of the historians Ben-Zion Dinur and Raphael Mahler. They all shared the desire to

---

1 *Major Trends*, p. 341.

Rivka Schatz

create a link between Hasidism and the period of Jewish national rebirth represented by Zionism. As Scholem put it:

> It is a well-known fact that the emotional world of Hasidism exercised a strong fascination upon men who were primarily concerned with the spiritual regeneration of Judaism. They soon perceived that the writings of the Hasidim contained more fruitful and original ideas than those of their rationalistic opponents, the *Maskilim*, and that the reborn Hebrew culture could find much of value in the heritage of Hasidism. Even so restrained a critic as Ahad Haam wrote around 1900, in a critical essay on modern Hebrew literature: 'To our shame we must admit that if today we want to find even a shadow of original Hebrew literature, we must turn to the literature of Hasidism; there, rather than in the literature of the *Haskala*, one occasionally encounters, in addition to much that is purely fanciful, true profundity of thought which bears the mark of the original Jewish genius.'[2]

The supporters of national rebirth attacked historians of the Jewish Enlightenment such as Graetz and Diaspora nationalists like Dubnow, who succeeded in denigrating Hasidism even when they were ostensibly praising it. However, this fervor to defend Hasidism produced historical distortions as well. The attempt to link Jewish culture to the movement of Jewish national rebirth, bridging the crisis of the *Haskala*, resulted in a loss of perspective. Is Hasidism truly a manifestation of Jewish rebirth? Can it really be described as the direct link between Judaism and the Jewish national and cultural revival, whose 'genes' were borne in a value-system produced by the 'original Jewish genius'? Some scholars at the beginning of the century, for example Samuel Joseph Ish-Horowitz, disagreed with the neo-romantic interpretation of Hasidism represented by Berdyczewsky and Buber. Ish-Horowitz argued unflinchingly that if any historical movement could be seen as a predecessor of Zionism, then a more likely candidate than Diaspora-oriented Hasidism was Sabbateanism, with its sweeping revolutionary vision. Ish-Horowitz described Sabbateanism as:

2   *Ibid.*, p. 326.

88

a national movement humanly inspired, the self-awakening to a desire to emerge from subjugation to redemption, from the dark ghetto to a Jewish state. How much human splendor, glory and greatness did it contain, enabling it to enthuse yearning hearts no longer able to bear the burden of exile and its material and moral hardships. ... Essentially, the goal of the Sabbatean movement was the same as that of the Zionist movement in our day. ... It was a beautiful and exalted human aspiration. It was the awakening of human emotion in the Jewish heart after long years of dormancy in exile, and Sabbetai Zevi was truly like Herzl in our generation. ... He opened up new vistas for 'those long disconsolate,' offering rest and comfort to those weary of tribulation and tired of exile.[3]

Horowitz's focus on Sabbateanism rather than Hasidism is understandable in a Herzlian Zionist; as a historical phenomenon, Sabbateanism surely has more in common with Zionism than does Hasidism. In fact, all those who sought to link Zionism and Hasidism, religious and secular thinkers alike, were constrained to emphasize its sociological nature as an intra-Jewish revolution with great creative vitality, directed against the structure of Diaspora society. In this, they claimed, it was prototypical of the pioneer Zionist society in Palestine. The religious-Zionist circles associated with the Mizrahi movement turned this approach into a quasi-scholarly pursuit, demonstrating that all the great hasidic rebbes were good Zionists as well.

The only one to internalize the hasidic system of values was Martin Buber, who sought to make of it a social and ideological model for Zionist education. In order to present it as such, he had to marshal considerable and multi-faceted interpretive skills. It was Buber who removed Hasidism from its historical context and turned it into a free-standing phenomenon. By sacrificing historicity for significance, he sought to transmit the 'message' of Hasidism to the new society in Palestine. Ish-Horowitz pointed out that this

---

3   S. Ish-Horowitz, *Ha-hasidut ve-ha-haskala*, Berlin 1911, p. 12.

neo-hasidic school of thought distorted the real nature of Hasidism, secularizing it in the spirit of the new humanism.[4]

I know of no interpretation other than Buber's that sought to mold the impact of Hasidism in the spirit of Jewish rebirth. Even Gershom Scholem, notwithstanding his quotation of Ahad Ha-Am, did not make any far-reaching claims for Hasidism's meaning for the cultural renewal sponsored by Zionism. On the contrary, the deeper Scholem delved into Buber's teachings, the further he fled from the Buberian 'message,' seeking instead the authentic historical and ideational content of Hasidism. Impelled by Buber's influence, he sought a translation of Hasidism into modern terms — but one that would not do violence to the precise meaning of its sources and the internal significance of its directions.

Scholem always sought a 'fixed standpoint'[5] by which to assess historical phenomena. This was provided by such Eastern European Jewish scholars as Buber and Zalman Shazar (the latter combined a scholarly career with an active role in Jewish politics, culminating in his term as President of the State of Israel). They gave Scholem a reliable perspective with which to begin his study, being, as he saw them, at one and the same time steeped in Jewish knowledge, endowed with the sweep of visionaries, and able to speak in contemporary Western terms. It was Shazar who influenced Scholem's attitude towards Sabbateanism and first aroused his interest in investigating it; and it was Buber who provided the point of departure for his study of Hasidism. Until the end of his life, Scholem returned again and again to his debate with Buber, who fascinated him as no one else. As he said:

> In Buber we have a deep and penetrating thinker who not only admires intuition in others but possesses it himself. He has that rare combination of a probing spirit and literary elegance which makes for a great writer. ... In one sense or another we are all his disciples. In fact most of us, when we speak about Hasidism,

4 *Ibid.* Horowitz's entire work is an attempt to uncover the 'real' Hasidism from beneath the layers of neo-romantic interpretation, and to negate any claims made in its name to be a model for modern Judaism.

5 'Reflections on Jewish Theology,' in *Jews and Judaism*, p. 261.

probably think primarily in terms of the concepts that have become familiar through Buber's philosophical interpretation.[6]

As Scholem saw it, Buber 'began as an enthusiastic admirer or even, one might say, adherent of religious mysticism,' who saw in Hasidism 'a mystic kernel of living Judaism.'[7] In this they had no quarrel; Scholem himself continued to describe Hasidism as 'mysticism at its best.' But Scholem could not accept Buber's hermeneutics, and it was ultimately not so much the neo-romanticism of Buber's mystical interpretations of the hasidic legends as their existential direction that aroused Scholem's deepest criticism. Buber's favorite maxim, that Hasidism is 'Kabbala become ethos,' continued to play a central role in Scholem's assessment of Hasidism, but the existential basis of that statement led Scholem to part ways with him. Buber's interpretation meant not only the de-gnostification of Hasidism, which severed a major link between Hasidism and earlier Kabbala; it also produced a redefinition, unacceptable to Scholem, of the hasidic ethos as a dialogue with 'the world as it is.'[8]

Scholem acknowledged the radicalism inherent in the teaching of Hasidism that God's presence fills the world, and in its conclusion that everything non-spiritual has a religious value. 'In *all* thy ways acknowledge Him,' taught the Baal Shem Tov, indicating that God was to be worshipped via both the spiritual and the material aspects of human life. However, Scholem differed sharply with Buber's inference that the corporeal world itself, what Buber called the 'here and now,' was sanctified. He was particularly annoyed by Buber's use of such extravagant formulations as 'life as it is' and 'concrete reality as it is,' which suggested a flirtation with the material world that Scholem did not find in hasidic writings. Scholem ascribed this intoxication with the concrete to Buber's own 'modernity.'[9]

6 'Martin Buber's Interpretation of Hasidism,' in *Messianic Idea*, pp. 229 ff.
7 *Ibid.,* p. 231.
8 *Ibid.,* p. 240. On Buber's interpretation of Hasidism see my article: 'Martin Buber, Master of Hasidic Teaching,' *Judaism,* IX (1960), pp. 277–280; and the introduction to my book, *Hasidism as Mysticism,* Princeton–Jerusalem 1993.
9 *Ibid.* See also 'Martin Buber's Conception of Judaism,'' in *Jews and Judaism*, pp. 165–170.

Scholem felt that Hasidism was idealistic rather than existential in this regard, focusing its gaze on the supernal rather than the material world. He asserted, rightly, that Hasidism speaks of the purification of life in order to achieve a 'life with God,' never forgoing the 'travails of love' inherent in every classical ethos. But Scholem's dissatisfaction with Buber's interpretation had another dimension as well. He himself was an idealist, an outlook he expressed clearly in his essay on Jewish theology,[10] in which he also attacked Buber's existentialist ideas and the distortions of Jewish theology to which they led.[11] According to Scholem, Buber's interpretation of Hasidism, too, stemmed from existential assumptions that neutralize such basic concepts as fear of God and belief in the validity of certain primary concepts, which cannot be translated into other categories without losing their authenticity. Scholem was unmoved by the 'beauty' and modernism of Buber's interpretation, which stripped Hasidism of its fundamental characteristics and obliterated its problematics with its monolithic approach. In contrast, Scholem's own phenomenological depiction allowed for nuances and complexities. Buber kept insisting on the 'message' and on seeing its purveyors as bearers of a new tiding. Scholem would have no part of that message or of Buber's humanistic passion for 'this world,' and he certainly did not believe that 'this world' had a following in Hasidism. His ear was attuned to the internal rhythm of the hasidic ethos, and he therefore attached far greater significance to the elements of dissociation from the world that he found in Hasidism than to any 'joyful affirmation of the here and now.'[12]

Scholem viewed Buber's attempt, as he put it, to bring God down into the human soul as a radically secular thesis, and he never identified with it. Scholem, in fact, did not like any sort of radicalism. Those radical features of Hasidism that he uneasily acknowledged were described as possibly belonging to the legacy of Sabbateanism. He was especially wary of such currents in modern religious Zionist thought, as exemplified by the ideas of R. Abraham Isaac Ha-Kohen

---

10 'Reflection on Jewish Theology,' in *Jews and Judaism*, pp. 261–297.
11 *Ibid.*, pp. 272–274.
12 *Messianic Idea*, pp. 240–241.

Kook. Scholem saw Kook's explication of the profane from the point of view of the sacred as continuing a trend towards a leveling of values, and as effacing the sharp gulf that had always separated the two realms in Judaism. In Scholem's analysis, the logic of such tendencies ultimately had a Sabbatean cast.

With the same thoroughness that he brought to his great work on Sabbateanism, Scholem began his study of Hasidism by clarifying the precise meaning of the concepts he found in its documents, in order to arrive at a depiction of its phenomenology. This process led straight to the heart of his debate with Buber. Thus, Scholem's clarification of the concept of 'worship in corporeality' (*'avoda ba-gashmiyut*) drew him to argue, against Buber, that ultimately, the 'message' of Hasidism revolves around 'divestment of corporeality' (*hitpashtut ha-gashmiyut*). In the same way, Scholem opposed Buber's interpretation of another central concept that Hasidism had absorbed from the Lurianic Kabbala, the doctrine of 'the uplifting of the sparks.' He rejected Buber's attempt to do away with the gulf between God and the world, or more precisely between 'life in God' and 'life in the world.' This was really a variation on the issue of *'avoda ba-gashmiyut*, but the eschatological–messianic element was now introduced, highlighting the contours of the debate. As Scholem explained,

> It is not the concrete reality of things that appears as the ideal result of the mystic's action, but something of the Messianic reality in which all things have been restored to their proper place in the scheme of creation. Thus, concepts like reality and concreteness mean something totally different for Buber than for the Hasidim.[13]

It was thus not only with Buber's 'here' but also with his 'now' that Scholem disagreed. For Buber, the human act itself was redemptive. Scholem understood, however, that Hasidism had not relinquished the eschatological dimension, and that, in its idealistic spirit, it saw the sparks as being raised to the 'true place' to which they belonged — their divine source. In this, of course, it also demonstrated

13 *Messianic Idea*, p. 243.

its continued connection with the kabbalistic 'gnosis,' from which Buber had 'liberated' it.

Neither Buber nor Scholem, however, accounted adequately for the striking new turn taken by Hasidism in emphasizing worship of God 'in all thy ways'; in the 'exaggerated' legitimation it gave to 'worship in corporeality' and to 'uplifting the sparks'; and in making all these equal in status to the classic modes of worship. Buber, had he been asked about the nature of this transformation, might have said that it stemmed from a change in the relative value attributed to the upper and lower worlds, so that the lower world had now acquired a status and value of its own. Scholem addressed the question indirectly; he seems to have viewed the change as a way of compensating for the people's loss of faith in the effectiveness of active messianism:

> Since, in addition, the Hasidim laid great stress on the teaching that human activity is not able really to bring about or reveal the Messianic world ... they were left, in their own view, only with prescribing ways and means for the individual to use the concrete as a vehicle to the abstract and thereby to the ultimate source of all being. Though couched in the language of very personal religion, this may be conventional theology and not nearly as exciting as the new interpretation which Buber has read into it.[14]

I cannot deny that I am unenthusiastic about the assumption that 'worship in corporeality' developed as compensation for a feeling of powerlessness in relation to the messianic process. I agree with Scholem that Hasidism is not to be considered a messianic movement, but I do not share the view that it was forced away from messianism by external factors. Scholem's above-quoted statement in this regard in fact seems to support the opinion of his opponents, who maintained that Hasidism did have a messianic element, which it was forced to conceal. I do not believe that movements grow by adopting one battle cry while believing another; and Hasidism fought for the sake of 'worship in corporeality' and not for the

14 *Ibid.*, p. 244.

messianic idea. If, however, what Scholem meant is that an inverse phenomenological correlation exists between these two elements, then it does seem that a movement lacking an acute messianic thrust will be open to the internalization of religious life and to finding ahistorical answers to its problems. It therefore seems sensible to view 'worship in corporeality' as a form of historical quietism.

It is difficult, on the basis of hasidic texts, to determine the overriding tone of their attitudes towards 'worship in corporeality.' Is it ceremonious, presenting such worship as a universal requirement, or apologetic, offering it rather as a possible alternative? The generation of the Baal Shem Tov displayed more missionary zeal in this regard, particularly in the context of its social revolt, which sought to bring 'theology' down to the popular level. The disciples of the Maggid of Mezritch, by contrast, clearly made an effort to limit the applicability of the demand for 'worship in corporeality,' endowing it with elitist features such as demands for great caution and special virtue in those who wished to perform it. This was a conscious flight from vulgarization — and perhaps from 'concrete reality as it is.'

Scholem also attacked Buber for disconnecting Hasidism from the traditional world of laws and commandments, demonstrating his anarchistic attitude towards tradition by emphasizing the form of the act at the expense of its content. He upbraided Buber for not ascribing the concept of sanctity to the commandments *per se*; Buber, he felt, had moved the issue to a different arena, as though Hasidism were concerned with moral responsibility only for how the act was performed, and not for the nature and content of the act itself. Scholem's own self-declared anarchism was of a different kind; it lay in the realm of authority[15] rather than in the realm of values. While he felt that values should be internalized rather than institutionalized, he showed his moderation by remaining faithful to their original meaning.

Scholem's debate with Buber has been discussed at some length here, both for its intrinsic interest and because of Buber's role in

---

15 See R. Schatz, 'Harut 'al ha-luhot — teologia be-siman mashber shel samkhut,' *Yedi'ot 'aharonot*, supplement in honor of G. Scholem on his eightieth birthday, December 2, 1977, pp. 4 and 6.

stimulating his research into Hasidism. While Scholem might well, ultimately, have shelved Buber's approach under the rubric of 'the price of existentialism in scholarship,' it raised basic questions that served to clarify his own views of the nature of Hasidism.

II

Scholem's study of Hasidism focused on two themes. One was its leaders, the *zaddiqim*, their personalities and religious experiences, and the other was the creativity of the movement's thinkers. Scholem was careful not to make unwarranted ascriptions of originality, and he always attempted to satisfy himself that he had been as precise as possible in distinguishing the truly innovative elements in Hasidism. As he said:

> It is not always possible to distinguish between the revolutionary and the conservative elements of Hasidism. ... The new elements must ... not be sought on the theoretical and literary plane, but rather in the experience of an inner revival.[16]

For Scholem, the crux of the matter was that

> the old ideas and conceptions, all of which duly make their appearance, have lost their stiffness and received a new infusion of life by going through the fiery stream of a truly mystical mind.[17]

An important aspect of the originality to be found in Hasidism lies in the fact that it was a popular movement and not merely a school of thought, and in that its thinkers confronted this popularism on a theoretical level. In two major articles of critical importance for an understanding of Hasidism, Scholem traced the lines by which Hasidism developed from a movement of religious revivalism to an institutionalized religious organization based on mysticism. These are '*Devequt*, or Communion with God'[18] and 'The Historic Persona of R. Israel Baal Shem-Tov.'[19] In these analyses of the central

16 *Major Trends*, p. 338.
17 *Ibid.*, p. 340.
18 In *Messianic Idea*, pp. 203–226.
19 *Devarim be-go*, pp. 287–324.

features of hasidic thought, Scholem discussed the contributions of two outstanding hasidic figures: the Baal Shem Tov, founder of the hasidic movement, and his disciple R. Dov Baer, the Maggid of Mezritch.

So much legendary material has been written about the Baal Shem Tov, the *zaddiq* from the Carpathians, that Scholem had first to prove that he was a real person. This he did by quoting from attacks on the Baal Shem Tov by his contemporary opponents in the 1740s — irrefutable proof that he must have existed! The distinction between history and legend is not always clear in hasidic sources about the Baal Shem Tov, and scholars had consequently been inclined to dismiss them. Scholem, however, evaluated the major documentary source about the Baal Shem Tov, *Shivhe ha-besht* (Praises of the Baal Shem Tov, first printed in the early nineteenth century), as containing material worthy of scholarly attention. For example, a close reading led him to conclude that the supposed participation of the Baal Shem Tov in a debate with the followers of the infamous pseudo-messiah Jacob Frank was never mentioned by his immediate disciples. This actually confirmed the scholarly view rejecting the historical foundation of the story.[20]

Scholem was the first scholar who dared to take the influence of a man like the Baal Shem Tov seriously. Scholem described him as

> making a deep and lasting impression on many by virtue of a unique combination of wonderworking capabilities and charisma, and his ability to make his words penetrate the hearts of the masses.[21]

While Martin Buber had presented the Baal Shem Tov as an exemplary figure, he nevertheless felt constrained to interpret away the magical connotation of his honorific name (the 'Good Keeper of the Divine Name'). Even the second and third generations of hasidic legends tended to rationalize the Baal Shem Tov's supernatural capabilities, attributing them to his penetrating insight and use of folk medicines. But Scholem, by emphasizing the 'undignified,'

20 *Ibid.*, pp. 305–307.
21 *Ibid.*, p. 324.

unelitist element of hasidic tradition, was able to confront and neutralize the unease that previous scholars had felt in dealing with a popular phenomenon. He thereby also clarified the guidelines framing the polemical writings of the Baal Shem Tov's disciple R. Jacob Joseph of Polnoye, the major source for traditions about the Baal Shem Tov.

In my opinion, however, Scholem overemphasized the element of sublimation in the Baal Shem Tov, and underemphasized what might be called the 'vulgar' mysticism evidenced in the role he attributed to the 'evil inclination' and in the social anarchism he displayed both personally and in his teachings. His solitary sojourns in the forest and his pointed visits to places not normally frequented by the learned and pious, as related in *Shivhe ha-besht*, were not merely ascetic customs. A tale found in one of the late traditions of the hasidic dynasty of Rizhyn indicates the sober view that the hasidim themselves took of the Baal Shem Tov. It is told that the disciples of R. Israel of Rizhyn, who was known for his regal style, asked him: 'May our rabbi explain to us how it is that the Baal Shem Tov lived simply and dwelt in the forests, while you [the Rizhyn dynasty] dwell in a palace and sit on a golden throne?' The rabbi answered: 'In the days of the Baal Shem, the robbers lived in the forest, so he too lived there. Today, the robbers dwell in palaces, and so I am here.'

The ethical tension inherent in the Baal Shem Tov's claim to the merits of the 'forbidden region' is too marked for us to ignore its problematic nature, even if we agree with Scholem in rejecting the Buberian interpretation of Hasidism as valuing the concrete *per se*. In fact, we may well ask whether the relative value of the concrete world is really the central problem of the study of Hasidism, or whether, rather, the issue is one of delimiting the periphery of the realm in which divine worship is possible, that is, the realm in which confrontation with the divine is permissible. This definition does not diminish the problems, but it relocates them from an ideational point of view.

In citing the Baal Shem Tov's teaching that 'man must desire the things of this world' in order to achieve true worship of God,[22]

22 *Ibid.*, p. 321.

Scholem summarized a major element of the new ethos advocating 'involvement' and 'experience,' without which nothing could be accomplished. A further element appears in another teaching of the Baal Shem Tov quoted by Scholem from a work called *Pe'er yesharim* by R. Pinhas of Koretz:

> A person may repair the world, and himself be infected with evil ... and this is what the Baal Shem Tov revealed ... that one must go down to Hell for God's sake, as the Talmud implies in saying, 'great is transgression in the name of God.' (BT *Nazir* 23b)[23]

It is surprising that Scholem failed to draw the conclusions inherent in this teaching, and ascribed the entire problematic and complex motif of 'descent for the sake of ascent' to the Maggid of Mezritch rather than to the Baal Shem Tov.[24] He seems not to have noticed the plentiful indications in the writings of Jacob Joseph of Polnoye that this motif was already present in the Baal Shem Tov's thought, thus denying the Baal Shem Tov his full degree of mystical extravagance. Moreover, I believe that there is another sort of mystical extravagance, belonging to the social realm, which Scholem missed entirely, though it emerges from a brief story that he himself cites from *Shivhe ha-besht*.[25] It is related that

> because of his *devequt* (communion with God), the Baal Shem Tov could not talk with people. His way of speaking was peculiar. His master [Ahijah of Shiloh] taught him to recite a chapter a day from 'Happy are they who are upright in their ways' [Psalm 119], ... and showed him wisdom, and so he came to be able to talk with people without ceasing his *devequt*.

Scholem's interpretation, that the Baal Shem Tov was not a gifted speaker, seems to miss the point. The crux of the story is, rather, how difficult it was to learn the technique of relating to other people

23 *Ibid.*, p. 310.
24 See R. Schatz, 'The Commentary of R. Israel Ba'al Shem Tov to Psalm CVII: The Myth and the Ritual of "The Descent to *Sheol*",' *Tarbiz*, XLII (1973/4), pp. 154 ff. (in Hebrew).
25 *Devarim be-go*, p. 311.

while in a state of *devequt*. The praxis the Baal Shem Tov was 'taught' clearly belongs to the earliest period of Hasidism.

The sources indicate that the doctrines of 'constant *devequt*' and of 'turning towards one's fellow-man' were given equal weight in Hasidism. Indeed, the Baal Shem Tov often taught that if one is addressed while at prayer, he should interrupt his communion with God in order to answer the speaker. There is more than a smattering of social extravagance at play here. Enlightenment historians had charged that the hasidic idea of the masses 'cooperating' with the elite, thus enabling the spiritual elevation of the latter, was no more that a dubious arrangement for exploiting the masses. Scholem agreed with the substance of their critique — 'Here,' he said, 'lies the perilous kernel of the doctrine of the *zaddiq*'[26] — but for some reason he exempted the Baal Shem Tov, who 'did not exploit his charisma for personal benefit.'[27] In this, Scholem's generosity towards the Baal Shem Tov did not fall short of that of the latter's own disciples, who put the emphasis on their master's unique ethos. As Zweifel astutely pointed out: 'It is surprising that in all their books, [the Baal Shem Tov's] holy disciples related almost nothing about signs and wonders, cures and talismans, but expatiated upon his holiness, his fear of God, his *devequt* and his fervor.'[28]

Nevertheless, by highlighting the foundations of the ostensibly classical ethic in the Baal Shem Tov's doctrine, Scholem demonstrated that the real nature of an ethic is determined by the historical circumstances in which it is realized. The value system may look the same as ever, but it is the way it operates in its context and the considerations determining the relative priority of its elements that demand the scholar's attention. As Scholem stated, 'The history of religion abounds in examples of such different evaluations of the same tenet under different historical conditions.'[29]

In Scholem's analysis, for example, *devequt* was not a static concept, but one that became revolutionary because of the changing circumstances in which it came to the fore. Well before the advent

---

26 *Ibid.*, p. 312.
27 *Ibid.*
28 E. Zweifel, *Shalom 'al yisrael*, Zhitomir 1868, p. 22a (in Hebrew).
29 *Messianic Idea*, p. 208.

of Hasidism, *devequt* was perceived as a more exalted spiritual state even than Torah study. However, this change in the Jewish scale of values created no widespread transformation, and aroused no massive opposition, until social circumstances arose to give it a radical, overpowering thrust — that is, until Hasidism adopted the ideal of *devequt* as the ideational framework for its revolutionary impetus. Similarly, the pantheistic idea that 'there is no place without God' occurs frequently in Jewish mystical literature from the time of the Zohar. Only when it became an overriding motif in the shift brought by Hasidism to religious life, however, did the Vilna Gaon begin to fear the consequences of its popularization, leading him to speak out against the Hasidim.

Scholem himself pointed to the tension that becomes apparent precisely when an idea becomes a dominant, living force. The point where 'renewers of the faith' demonstrate spiritual radicalism will always be controversial, because of the vulgarization attendant upon the very effort to popularize their ideas. 'If you turn aside from your *devequt*, you will have become idolaters,' taught the Baal Shem Tov, interpreting the biblical injunction not to 'turn aside and worship other gods' (Deut. 11:16). Scholem pointed out that the very radicalism of this demand 'already contained the germ of decay, a dialectic typical of radical and spiritualist movements.'[30] Drinking spirits and smoking 'lolky' would now gain an equal status with contemplating the letters of the prayers as means of attaining *devequt*.

Scholem did not take note of the critique in this vein leveled against Hasidism's spiritual radicalism by the conservative intelligentsia of the contemporary Jewish world. *Nefesh ha-hayyim* by Rabbi Hayyim b. Isaac (1749–1821), founder of the renowned yeshiva of Volozhin, is the most poignant in its analysis of the spiritual direction taken by Hasidism, and in its understanding of the internal dialectic involved. Rabbi Hayyim was deeply versed in Kabbala and an outspoken opponent of Hasidism. In his view, spiritualism had become the enemy of normative Judaism.[31] He rejected the hasidic

30 *Ibid.*, p. 209.
31 I find it baffling that *Nefesh ha-hayyim* (Vilna 1824) continues to be treated as just another work in the kabbalistic corpus, when it is actually a crusade

reinterpretation of the rabbinic demand to study the Torah 'for its own sake' (*lishma*) as signifying 'for the sake of God's mystical name.' The Torah, he insisted, must be studied 'without any other motive,' and to take this view was a true sign of belonging to the mystical elite, which allowed itself so stringent an interpretation that anyone who deviated could not be considered a *Hasid* — that is, a man of piety. This, in fact, was the original, authentic hasidic interpretation, in the spirit of the Baal Shem Tov, of the injunction not to 'turn aside and worship other gods.'[32] Rabbi Hayyim stressed the tension that had since developed in Hasidism between study and *devequt*, and expressed his opposition to the hasidic rites of 'purification of thought' before the performance of commandments. 'The practice of Torah and commandments,' he declared, 'is not necessarily a function of great *kavvana* (concentration) and true *devequt*.' He cautioned that to carry out a commandment solely for the sake of its mystical intention might actually be to break it; the point of the divine law was to carry it out in the sense and form in which it was given. According to Rabbi Hayyim, to do something 'for the sake of Heaven' was not a value in and of itself. *Devequt*, for him, was not a mystical exercise; it meant purity of thought, in the rational sense, in Torah study.[33]

Scholem was right in emphasizing that the statements of the Baal Shem Tov himself do not exhibit that craving for the mystical Naught, that 'degree of abandonment to emotionalism that has no precedent'[34] known as the loss of self in mystical intoxication. But he did have tremendous religious enthusiasm; the movements of his body at prayer were, in his words, like those of a drowning man thrashing about to save himself and grasping at every straw. 'I must thank God,' he said, 'that I am still alive after prayer.' His prayers

against Hasidism, without mentioning it by name. In his introduction, the author's son relates that his father begged him shortly before his death to see that this book was published before all his other writings; however, 'the great scholars of the generation' insisted on publishing his other works first.

32 See *Messianic Idea*, p. 209.
33 *Nefesh ha-hayyim, Part I, chaps. 21–22.*
34 *Messianic Idea*, p. 214.

were more of a cry to heaven than a quest for *unio mystica*, in contrast to the Maggid of Mezritch, who portrays such union as the ultimate goal. As Scholem said of the Maggid, 'He is the ascetic whose gaze is fixed on, or, I might rather say, lost in God. He is a mystic of unbridled radicalism and singularity of purpose.'[35]

Gershom Scholem singled out many additional issues crucial to the study of Hasidism, a field in which, more than any other area of Jewish mysticism, the problems themselves require definition and clarification. Where 'Kabbala becomes ethos,' its path becomes tangled. The literature, encompassing over two hundred years of creativity, is vast. Scholem saw, however, that the great struggle of Hasidism, ultimately, was to enable its devotees to come out of the 'spiritual desert' and attain those great hours of joy when the heart overflows in divine service; it 'transformed the lowest forms of activity into something of a higher order.'[36] With characteristic sensitivity, Scholem felt the pulse that vitalized Hasidism, reading between the lines of its thinkers, listening enthralled to its legends, and ever symphathetic its aspirations.

---

35 *Devarim be-go*, p. 348.
36 *Messianic Idea*, pp. 220–221.

GERSHOM SCHOLEM'S CONCEPTION
OF JEWISH NATIONALISM

by

Nathan Rotenstreich*

I

THE EXCELLENCE of Gershom Scholem's scholarly, historical and interpretive oeuvre in his chosen discipline has relegated his views on Jewish nationalism to the sidelines of scholarly attention. However, a connection exists between his scholarly work and his national thought, not only because his roots in Judaism and the Jewish people drew him to both concerns, but also because of the influence of his scholarly endeavor upon his understanding of the place of the Jewish people in the contemporary world and its national and cultural future. Moreover, it was his national thought that enabled him to formulate non-dogmatic interpretations of Jewish phenomena, past and present. The same cannot always be said of currently prevailing modes of scholarship, where, quite frequently, norms applied to the present and future result in ideological interpretations of the past, or, conversely, interpretations of the past give a defined thrust to inquiries into the present and predictions for the future. Where Scholem is concerned, his openness to the significance of past manifestations of Judaism — although it did have its limitations — enabled him to maintain a reciprocal relationship between his scholarly studies of the past and his analysis of present events, with a view to arriving at normative conclusions for the future.

The essays collected in the Hebrew volume *Devarim be-go* (many of which have appeared in translation in *On Jews and Judaism*

* Nathan Rotenstreich is Emeritus Professor of Philosophy at The Hebrew University of Jerusalem and Vice President of the Israel Academy of Sciences and Humanities.

in Crisis) provide our principal sources for clarifying and tracing Scholem's conception of the Jewish people and Jewish nationalism. For further light on these issues, we may turn to his analyses of the status of the Jewish people within German culture and its position *vis-à-vis* the German nation.

II

Let us begin our inquiry by focusing on the relationship between Scholem's ideas and those of Ahad Ha-Am (Asher Ginsberg, 1856–1927), who established the branch of Zionism that envisioned the land of Israel as the cultural rather than political center of world Jewry. The views of Ahad Ha-Am were influential in motivating Scholem's ideological and practical involvement in the 'Berit Shalom' movement for Jewish-Arab conciliation (1925–c. 1935). Asked in an interview whether his opposition to the idea that Israel should aspire to be 'like all the other nations' indicated that he identified with Ahad Ha-Am's ideology, Scholem replied with a declaration both autobiographical and analytic:

> Correct. In this respect I am an Ahad Ha-Amist and religious, but more religious than Ahad Ha-Am. I don't believe in a world of total secularism in which the religious factor will not manifest itself with redoubled strength.[1]

In a lead article in *She'ifotenu*, the ideological organ of Berit Shalom, Scholem also makes use of Ahad Ha-Am's well-known statement that Zionism has a vital role to play in solving the problem of Judaism, even if it does not have the power to solve the problem of the Jews.[2]

However, Scholem seems to have gone beyond this formulation even in his early, Berit Shalom period, and all the more so in his later years. Following the Six-Day War, Scholem said that

> one of the tragedies of our effort [to promote mutual understanding with the Arabs] is that those Arabs who occasionally

---

1 *Jews and Judaism*, p. 34.
2 *She'ifotenu*, Elul 1931, p. 185; the article is unsigned but was written by Scholem.

approached us, and with whom fruitful dialogue seemed possible, were without exception silenced by overt terror, or in truth, by murder.[3]

He saw it as a great honor to have been a member of Berit Shalom, but added that while this group did not err in its humanity, it may have erred in its political platform.[4] This critical distinction allowed Scholem to continue seeking to preserve the element of humanity, while abandoning the specific policy envisioned by Berit Shalom concerning political accommodation with the Arab world. It would seem — and this is based on conversations with Scholem rather than on published evidence — that he viewed the partition plan submitted by the Peel Commission in 1937 as a crossroads. Its human significance was that it allowed for the two nations, Jewish and Arab, to co-exist not together but side by side, and it was therefore both realistic and humane.

Scholem thus acknowledged the importance of the political element. In a speech given in Zurich after the Six-Day War, he declared:

> We must struggle for external conditions in the political sphere which allow us to determine the internal fate of our nation, for which we alone are responsible.[5]

The political realm neither encompassed nor exhausted the national aspirations of the Jews; but national existence in the intrinsic sense, or rebirth, was impossible in the absence of appropriate external conditions. This conviction is not confuted by his autobiographical testimony that, for him, the decision for Zionism was ethical rather than political,[6] even though a decision made on this basis might lead people to draw political conclusions as well. The choice for Zionism was 'a decision to return to ourselves, and consciously integrate ourselves into the continuum of the history of Israel and take the responsibility for our lives into our own hands on all levels ... as

3 *Devarim be-go*, p. 131.
4 *Ibid.*, p. 121.
5 *Ibid.*, p. 130.
6 *Jews and Judaism*, p. 2.

Jews, and as Jews alone.'[7] The ethical decision thus had to do with a return to responsibility, and to an awareness of continuity between present and past. In the final analysis, this return could not take place without a political order to provide an external framework for the realization of the ethical decision. Scholem's emphasis on the personal aspect of the ethical decision gives an additional dimension to Ahad Ha-Am's formulation, while in no way contradicting it.

III

In an article entitled 'In What Do They Differ,' which interestingly enough appeared in the same issue of *She'ifotenu*,[8] Scholem bursts the bounds of the various Zionist formulations inherited from the founding generation of Zionism, including Ahad Ha-Am. He states and here he is unconcerned with separating the problem of the Jews from the problem of Judaism that Zionism is the guarantee, 'by an extraordinary historical effort, not merely that the miserable existence of the Jews will be continued from one generation to the next, but that it will be secured once and for all.'[9] In this formulation, Zionism is not a matter of relocating Jewish existence from one set of conditions to another; it is a historical watershed, and the emphasis on the radical nature of the change is accompanied by a parallel emphasis on the wretchedness of Jewish existence heretofore.

Moreover, Ahad Ha-Am's doctrine involved an optimistic vision of a spiritual center in the land of Israel inspiring Jewish national culture in the Diaspora. In fact, says Scholem, the historical dynamic of the Zionist movement was leading it, despite itself, more towards an embodiment of the conception of the twentieth-century Jewish historian Simon Dubnow (using the name, as he says, in a symbolic sense) — that is, towards the establishment merely of yet another Jewish center demanding some sort of independent status for itself in the historical succession of autonomous Jewish centers, which Dubnow saw as the regnant pattern of Jewish history in the Diaspora.[10]

7 *Devarim be-go*, p. 128.
8 Reprinted in G. Scholem, *Od davar*, Tel Aviv 1989, pp. 74–82.
9 *Ibid.*, p. 76.
10 *Ibid.*, pp. 78–79.

Scholem saw a paradox here, one that would seem to apply both to political Zionism and to the Zionism of Ahad Ha-Am. The vital forces awakened by Zionism were being poured into pre-existing molds, represented by the Jewish communities of the Diaspora; and while this might ensure the continuity of Jewish existence for another generation or two, it could not vouchsafe it the permanent guarantee that Scholem saw as essential to Zionism. This led to a distancing from the initial and authentic impetus of Zionism, for which Zionism itself was paradoxically responsible.[11]

Although this article was written in 1931, Scholem's observations are just as cogent today: under present circumstances, the State of Israel seems to act more as a conservative factor maintaining the status quo than as the catalyst for a new Jewish reality. But the significance of Scholem's statements lies not only in the strength of his analysis, but also in their expression of the ethical foundation of his approach to Zionism, which led him to take a radical view of the Zionist mission. In this regard it is immaterial whether he felt himself, from an autobiographical point of view, to be closer to the ideas of Ahad Ha-Am than to other versions of classical Zionism. It is the foundation of his own orientation towards Zionism that informs his vision and analysis.

IV

Scholem's remarks about World War One and his refusal to serve in the German army are notable in this context. He says that he was not a pacifist: he wanted to learn to shoot, but not to fight for Germany.[12] Taking his denial of pacifism beyond the events of World War One and his attitude towards them, it may be that we can apply the distinction between pacifism and humanism to his stance on Zionist-Arab relations. It was humanism, not pacifism, that motivated Scholem to support the position of Berit Shalom, and it continued to motivate him even after he had abandoned that position. 'Our nation has proved that it knows how to fight,' he said after the Six-Day War, 'but how pathetic is the state of a world in

11 *Ibid.*, pp. 76–77.
12 *Jews and Judaism*, p. 16.

which this proof earned us more respect and admiration than the nurturing of those unique gifts of peace for which the State of Israel was founded.'[13] 'Peace for Israel' naturally includes peace with the Arabs, and it was Scholem's hope that hatred and enmity would eventually be transformed into mutual understanding, respect and friendship.[14]

V

Scholem's analysis of the status of the Jewish people within the historical reality of the last few generations was decisively influenced by his personal experiences as a German Jew, and by his analytical assessment of the situation of Germany Jewry in relation to its surroundings. These led him away from the idea that the status of the Jews could be resolved simply by reformulating attitudes towards Judaism. Scholem's position is reflected in his response to the views of the Orthodox thinker Isaac Breuer, who based his argument against Zionism on the theology of his illustrious forebear, Samson Raphael Hirsch, the foremost nineteenth-century exponent of Orthodoxy in Germany. In a review of Breuer's *New Kusari*,[15] Scholem points to the ambivalence inherent in Hirsch's slogan, *Torah 'im derekh eretz* ('Torah with secular culture'), which envisioned the ideal Jew as a Torah-observant, enlightened person of culture. He categorizes this theology as one of 'bourgeois accommodation,' which brought about a devaluation of the Jewish essence. It is this principle of accommodation in its various expressions and forms that was, in Scholem's analysis, the axis of German Jewry's way of life, and this in turn was a microcosm of Diaspora Jewry in the modern world.

The obverse side of such accommodation was German Jewry's self-delusion — the butt, as Scholem depicted it, of Zionism's rebellion,[16] whether it was seen as a moral imperfection, reflecting the community's lack of self-awareness, or as an intellectual flaw, reflecting its failure to heed the imperative of self-knowledge. The

---

13 *Devarim be-go*, p. 130.
14 *Ibid.*, p. 132.
15 'The Politics of Mysticism: Isaac Breuer's New Kuzari,' in *Messianic Idea*, pp. 325–334.
16 *Jews and Judaism*, p. 2.

Jews believed that they were achieving a harmonic symbiosis with German culture and becoming partners in German national life, even going so far as to begin a propaganda campaign for Jewish absorption into German culture, and thence into the German people. But they were fatally mistaken in this regard, because it was not the Jews themselves who won the struggle for their civil rights, but a critical and — at the time – victorious stratum of non-Jews who won it in their behalf.[17] Casting off Jewish history for German history, preoccupied with currying the favor of the German environment, the Jews could never achieve their hearts' desire. Their unflagging attempts to come closer to their non-Jewish surroundings would never, ultimately, bring them to a safe harbor, either in daily human terms or from a cultural-historical perspective.

One of the hallmarks of German-Jewish myopia was the romanticized interpretation they gave to the surrounding culture in its various manifestations. Their relationship with the works of Friedrich Schiller, the German poet who was spokesman for the noblest human ideals, was more real to them than the encounter with their German contemporaries[18]. This romanticization of creative works emanating from the non-Jewish environment served only to deepen their self-delusion; for literary and philosophical expressions could not be made to take the place of real life, which continued on its empirical course, heedless of the classical expressions represented by Schiller. In their widely differing ways, both the Orthodox theologian Hirsch and the neo-Kantian philosopher Hermann Cohen were examples of this kind of chimerical accommodation. Scholem said of Cohen that he represents a 'shocking' chapter in German-Jewish history,[19] and called 'tragicomic' the great Jewish philosopher's hailing of the acquittal of Dreyfus as a messianic event.

Moreover, we cannot but see that 'the disdain in which so many Germans held the Jews fed on the ease with which the upper cultural stratum of the Jews disavowed its own tradition.'[20] This attempt to shake off their Judaism did not pay off, 'for it was precisely this desire

17 *Ibid.*, p. 75.
18 *Ibid.*, p. 79.
19 *Ibid.*, pp. 63–64.
20 *Ibid.*, p. 76.

on the part of the Jews to be absorbed by the Germans that hatred understood as a destructive maneuver against the life of the German people.'[21] Even in circles where this demonological interpretation had no footing, 'where Germans ventured on a discussion with Jews in a humane spirit, such a discussion ... was always based ... on the progressive atomization of the Jews as a community in a state of dissolution.'[22] The Germans saw no room here for ethnic or cultural symbiosis, because they did not see cultured Jewish society as a prospective partner in such a process. There was thus a complex of factors and attitudes at work in the relationship between German Jews and the non-Jewish world, and Scholem, it seems, saw this as paradigmatic for all of Diaspora Jewry. Their longstanding proximity to their neighbors produced a cycle of reactions on both sides, which served to propel the Jews further along the self-deceptive path they had followed in their attempt to come to terms with their environment.

Though Scholem himself had distinguished in his article in *She'ifotenu* between the problem of the Jews and the problem of Judaism, this distinction is not brought to bear on his integrative view of the fate of German Jewry — and, perforce, on that of the entire Jewish nation. If recent Jewish history was characterized by the erosion of Jewish culture and tradition, it was marked no less by the constant deterioration of day-to-day relationships between Jews and their environment. The question of Judaism and the Jewish question were a single complex that constituted the overriding manifestation of the Diaspora Jewish experience. Scholem counterposed the Diaspora Jew's constant presence in a foreign environment with the normative idea that the Jew ought to be confronting himself, his own people and his own roots. In this regard the personal problem of the individual and that of the community as a whole were one.[23]

VI

Scholem emphasized that it is ultimately an ethical decision that propels the struggle for liberation from this vicious cycle of

21 *Ibid.*, p. 90.
22 *Ibid.*, p. 62.
23 *Ibid.*, p. 23.

self-deception, atomization and dependence on a rejecting environment. This basic ethical motivation is more authentic than political evaluations of one sort or another, and exists at a level that transcends political motivations.

It is from this perspective that we must view Scholem's sketch of Russian Jewry, a description so antithetical to his depiction of German Jewry that it seems almost an idealization. 'Russian Jewry lived in a state of material hardship and was prey to decrees and persecutions. ... Despite this, or perhaps because of it, Russian Jewry was outstanding in mental fecundity, in unbounded idealistic enthusiasm, soaring imagination and unusual sensitivity,' and in what Scholem ironically calls 'a Jewish variation of Russian *nichevo* [nothing].'[24] His use of the latter phrase hints to us that acceptance of the ethos of the environment did not necessarily invite the negation of Jewish existence or of its cultural essence. On the contrary, the negation of *nichevo* could be taken in the sense of overcoming distressing circumstances to bring about an independent spiritual fruition.

Moreover, Russian Jewry — and this was true not only of the Zionists, but also of the other Russian Jewish movements — conducted its quest for full citizenship rights not on the individual level, but as a national group.[25] Its aspirations were thus essentially opposed to the atomizing trend that characterized German Jewry and Western European Jewry in general. It is not accidental that the leaders of the various schools of Palestine-oriented Zionism, including the political leaders of the Palestine Jewish community, came from Russia. They felt a bond to the community, which they continued seeking to express even after the Jews had abandoned the effort to gain a position in or *vis-à-vis* their existing environment and had begun looking to establish, as it were, their own environment. This bond with the Jewish community, rather than the attempt to deal with the Jewish question in Herzl's sense, is what Scholem sees as the continuity between Russian Jewry and the Zionist endeavor. This gives us a clue to Scholem's view of the essence of Zionism,

24 *Devarim be-go*, p. 124.
25 *Ibid.*, p. 126.

over and above the different historical or social conditions in which it grew.

VII

Scholem's integrative analysis of the condition of the Jewish nation in recent generations leads into his approach to Zionism. His emphasis on the ethical aspect of the individual's choice for Zionism indicates his conceptualization of that choice as a return of the individual to himself, or as an assumption of responsibility for his own destiny. The next step is the shouldering of responsibility by the community, composed of individuals, for its own fate. The central theme in Scholem's discussions of Zionism is not the return of the nation to its land, but its return to the plane of history, 'which means the acceptance of responsibility for itself, its achievements and its failures.' It is in this context that Scholem speaks of activity in the political dimension of secular history[26] — a point deserving of our attention, for Scholem did not accept the secular interpretation of Jewish reality that was to emerge from Zionism, as we shall discuss below.

The entry of the Jews into modern history does not signify — at least, not in the simple sense — the return of the Jewish people to its history and the resumption of its *Heilsgeschichte*. Entry into the historical dimension means involvement in the process of events from this time on, including the absorption of structures that history has called forth or that have become commonplace in the course of history, such as the territorial-national structure and its various trappings. This definition draws clear boundaries, in content and in time, between messianism and Zionism. Scholem says of Zionism that it is a process, 'a most legitimate process. Zionism is not a messianic movement. And that is its secret. Because as a messianic movement it [would be] doomed in advance to failure.'[27] The emphasis is on the process: the historical realm is one of continuous, ceaseless process, whereas messianism represents both the eschatological end of the process and the stage leading up to this culmination.

26 *Jews and Judaism*, p. 44.
27 *Ibid.*, p. 43.

If history is to be understood, to use Whitehead's phrase, as 'taking time seriously,' then Zionism is 'a most legitimate process' and is to be grasped neither, on the one hand, as a successor to the messianic movements of the past or a perpetuation of the messianic element in Judaism, nor, on the other, as a preparatory stage for the realization of messianic expectations. It is not that religious redemption is excluded from Scholem's field of vision, but the redemption of the Jewish nation to which he aspires as a Zionist is not to be identified with it. The ethical expression of existence on the historical plane is the acceptance of historical responsibility *vis-à-vis* oneself and others, without messianic pretensions: 'Action on the political plane of secular history is something different from action on the spiritual-religious plane. It would be disastrous to confuse the two'[28] — and this is so, we might add, even though the messianic hope is widely interpreted as requiring the end of the subjugation of the Jews to foreign powers. In this connection, Scholem mentions his fear of a growing new Sabbateanism, blurring the essential difference between Zionism as entry into the historical plane and messianism as a concern with the apocalypse.

The entry into history is not a leap or an idyllic process. On the contrary, it has an element of danger, and Scholem therefore called it 'a calculated risk.' It involves secularization as an integral 'part of the process of our entry into history,'[29] and Scholem recognized that the people had accepted this element, with all its implications. However, he took issue with two opposing attitudes arising in this context: one, mentioned above, is the comprehension of Zionism as a continuation of messianism, which negates the independence of the historical dimension; the other is the view that the entry into history abrogates other frames of reference that are not realized in this process, particularly that of religion or faith. The entry into history may have brought the co-existence of these different frames of reference into sharper perspective, but this does not mean that the historical frame of reference, either by definition or by virtue of the possibilities it opens up, cancels out the others. To be sure,

28 *Ibid.*, pp. 44–45.
29 *Ibid.*, p. 34.

to the degree to which we acknowledge historicity, we must also acknowledge secularity. But, just as historicity does not encompass the diversity of reality, either in human or in cosmic terms, so secularism cannot be taken as a factor or direction capable of describing all of reality.

In the era of emancipation, the Jews had fought 'not for the sake of their rights as a people, but for the sake of assimilating themselves to the peoples among whom they lived.'[30] Zionism, on the other hand, is the struggle of the nation for its political and human rights as such — and, we might add, not among the nations but over against or alongside them. The determination of the unique identity of the Jews leads into a discussion of secularism and its potential, or of faith and its nature, and the relation of each to the course taken by the Jewish nation.

VIII

As noted earlier, Zionism, seen as the movement of revival of the Jewish nation within concrete reality, signifies the entry of the Jewish nation into the process of history. But being exposed to processes does not mean being swept along by them. Scholem's emphasis on the nation's responsibility for itself stems partly from his recognition of the problematic nature of two aspects of the entry into history: for one thing, the process of history has a broad or universal sweep that is not confined to the particular concerns of the people entering into it; for another, not all that it brings to pass is necessarily binding or normative. Scholem sought the retention of the Jewish norm, as he understood it, within the historical process rather than in opposition to it, and that is why considerations of religion and faith arose in connection with — and for the sake of — the rebirth of the Jewish nation.

Although Scholem himself did not formulate this explicitly, we may infer that entry into history does not mean accepting the authority of modernism, if this entails secularism or declaring the absolute autonomy of the individual — that is, attempting to shape human existence using human resources alone. Neither does the

---

30 *Ibid.*, p. 77.

entry into history mean attempting to be 'like all the other nations'; on the contrary, it signifies the people's quest for its own unique path within history. Scholem's statements in this connection are revealing of his own spiritual world, and they shed light on the spiritual background to his scholarly work, including his study of Kabbala:

> I have never cut myself off from God. I don't understand atheists; I never did. I think atheism is understandable only if you accept the rule of unbridled passions, a life without values. I am convinced that there is no morality that has any inner meaning unless it has a religious basis. I don't believe there is such a thing as the absolute autonomy of man, whereby man makes himself and the world creates itself.[31]

We ought to interpret this programmatic statement very carefully. It speaks not only of the idea of individual autonomy, but also of the idea of a self-cosmogony, of the cosmos generating itself. Both attitudes are rejected, because of their common claim that the realms to which they refer, the human and the cosmic respectively, are of independent origin and status. Scholem is not referring to individual autonomy in the sense expressed, for example, by Kant — that is, to self-legislation of a rational nature. His concern is with the clash between human beings as creatures of instinct and the values or principles that guide humanity as such. Scholem rejects autonomy because he believes that the realm of values cannot be sustained without a relationship to a transcendent God, or, from the opposite perspective, that there is no such thing as free-standing values, and that values are not simply an aspect of human reason. Scholem's rejection of secularism in the sense of secular modernism is not founded on — or not solely on — the internal norms of Jewish culture; its basis is metaphysical, and it turns on the relationship between the realm of values or ethics to the human sphere.

Scholem states: 'I ... thought that perhaps there is a hidden facet to the historical process taking place here that may have a religio-metaphysical aspect.'[32] Since the realm of history is not

31 *Ibid.*, p. 35.
32 *Ibid.*, p. 43.

sealed, it can also be deciphered in terms of an inner principle that is perhaps revealed only to one whose concern centers on the metaphysical perspective, where the visible realms are not identified with the entirety of factual or normative reality. It may be said that the contemplation of historical processes leads the observer to the meta-historical realm, while the metaphysical distinction between historicity and autonomy in the secular sense is what allows for the differentiation between the visible and the hidden.

This orientation towards the hidden is reinforced by a basic idea that goes beyond the normative element given such emphasis in Scholem's remarks on atheism, cited above. 'If you ask me, I say that the kabbalists had a fundamental feeling that there is mystery — a secret — in the world. The world is also — but not only — what is apparent to us.'[33] To claim autonomy, whether in the individual domain or the cosmic (if we may apply the term to this sphere), or to claim the independence of history and the cosmos — any such attitude implies a negation of the hidden dimension and denies the principle of mystery. But the transcendent always lies in the realm of mystery, and Scholem therefore points to the contrast between the hidden and the visible. The latter is represented or embodied by technology, which is not only the complex of machines and tools wielded by human beings; it signifies the attitude that human beings can control the universe from within their own human bounds and within the bounds of the visible universe — making the universe, in this sense, subject to man.

The source of the Kabbala is mentioned in this context because the hidden dimension cannot be deciphered or even expressed except in symbols, the only possible expression of mystery, though they do not pretend to encompass the hidden dimension. 'The kabbalists were symbolists,' says Scholem, and in a statement both descriptive of the mystics' world and revealing of its fascination for him, he adds: 'What attracts you here to the kabbalists — in any case, what attracts me — is that a rather small group of people were able to create symbols that expressed their personal situation as a world

33 *Ibid.*, p. 48.

situation.'[34] The symbol thus serves as a sort of bridge between man and the universe, even as the individual realizes that it does not comprehend the mystery, either of his own existence or of that of the universe beyond. As he expressed most clearly in his 'Ten Unhistorical Aphorisms,' the category of symbol was central to Scholem's thought and to his interpretation of the essential nature of the Kabbala, above and beyond the diversity of its historical manifestations.[35]

From both the personal and the theoretical point of view, the meeting of the different strands of Scholem's inner world becomes evident here. For him, there were conceptual motivations to support the existential decision to seek a rebirth of the Jewish nation in the present, and conceptual motivations also informed his view that this decision was not meant to restrict the Jew's being to the confines of the visible world. The Kabbala serves as a sort of historical representative of a thrust that is both metaphysical and historical, of the relation between mystery and symbol; it may be understood as the factual, literary and aesthetic expression of how that relation can be seen. One might say that it is the symbol of the connection between the visible and the hidden. There is thus an affinity between Scholem's personal return to the sources of religion and faith and his scholarly interest in Kabbala, although this does not imply that he regarded Kabbala as the future culture of the Jewish nation. Scholem's thoughts on the Jewish people seem to have enriched his scholarly involvement with the Kabbala, without his scholarship dictating a dogmatic or doctrinaire approach to the possible role of Kabbala in the future.

IX

Three statements that Scholem made on various occasions seem appropriate to conclude our discussion of his conception of Jewish nationalism. Quoting Chaim Weizmann's famous remark to the Peel Commission, 'He who remembers has right [i.e., historical rights],'

---

34 *Ibid.*

35 On the place of the symbol in Scholem's thought, see N. Rotenstreich, 'Symbolism and Transcendance — On Some Philosophical Aspects of Gershom Scholem's Opus,' *Review of Metaphysics*, June 1978, pp. 604 ff.

Scholem declared: 'Memory is one of the mighty forces in the life of the Jews. From now on a tremendous urge to rehabilitate our land, to reconstruct it, will be added.'[36] In his debate with Isaac Breuer, Scholem asserted: 'Only he who can change is master of the future.' Both of these statements are linked to his fundamental view of the Zionist idea as signifying entry into history, referring both to the relationship between past and present and to that between present and future. Finally, Scholem summarizes the sense or experience of relating to mystery by saying: 'If humanity should ever lose the feeling that there is mystery — a secret dimension — in the world, then it's all over with us. But I don't believe we'll ever come to that.'[37]

Only by bringing together these various aspects of Scholem's thought, and by examining their context and the dialectic between them, can we shed light on Scholem's views on the issues of Jewish nationhood in recent generations and the place this chapter occupies within the general framework of his thought.

36 *Devarim be-go*, p. 129.
37 *Jews and Judaism*, p. 48.

GERSHOM SCHOLEM AS BIBLIOPHILE

by

Malachi Beit-Arié*

I

MUCH ATTENTION has been focused on the breadth and depth of Gershom Scholem's scholarly oeuvre. His contributions to Judaic Studies, and to the movement for national rebirth, have been discussed by others. This article is concerned with a lesser-known sphere of Scholem's scholarly pursuits: his lifelong interest in the scaffolding with which he built the magnificent and enduring edifice of his scholarship, that is, his exuberant passion for books. Can a portrait of Gershom Scholem omit the thousands of books he loved, which surrounded him in his study? Can his personality be depicted without including his feverish enthusiasm for assembling every printed item bearing even indirectly on the literature of mysticism, Kabbala, Sabbateanism and Hasidism? No other modern scholar of Judaic Studies has dealt so extensively with bibliography, has based his research on such vast bibliographical knowledge or has displayed such remarkable expertise in the history of Hebrew printing and typography.

Although bibliographical research remained an aid to Scholem's scientific work, rather than a science in and of itself, it held a special charm and fascination for him. His interest in handwritten and printed books went beyond their function as the sole sources of the historian (as he always preferred to define himself), as the laboratory materials to be dissected by the student of the history of ideas with his philological scalpel. He had a unique sort of emotional

---

* Malachi Beit-Arié is Professor of Codicology and Palaeography at The Hebrew University of Jerusalem.

120

relationship with books, where the distinctions between function and essence, between the vessel and its contents, became blurred. Scholem's love for books was marked by such abandon and almost sensual enthusiasm that some observers were misled. Speaking on the occasion of Scholem's sixtieth birthday in 1958, S.Y. Agnon told of the esteem in which the Jewish philosopher Franz Rosenzweig had held the young scholar, whom he knew before his immigration to Palestine. Rosenzweig praised Scholem 'for his knowledge, for his precision about sources, and because in everything he strove to get to the primary source, for his critical sense and for the strength of his memory, and for his ability to break through outer shells and reach the core.'[1] When Agnon once visited Rosenzweig after Scholem had been to call, Rosenzweig remarked to him: 'I believe he [Scholem] may become a sacrifice to the bibliography of the Kabbala. But,' he added, 'the sacrifice is worthy of the altar.' According to Agnon's interpretation, 'perhaps Rosenzweig meant to say that Jewish mysticism was worthy of Scholem's sacrificing himself to it, even if only to list its books for the scholars to come after him.'[2] Scholem, of course, went far beyond 'listing' in his great and multi-faceted scholarly endeavor, but he always viewed the books themselves as the noble and graceful cornerstones of his work.

Scholem traced the paths by which spiritual creativity was disseminated by systematically investigating the distribution of kabbalistic literature and of Hebrew texts in general, printed material as well as manuscript copies. He thereby uncovered some fascinating chapters in the history of Jewish culture. The place of books in Scholem's inner world can be likened to the place of symbols in the Kabbala: Just as the spiritual reality represented by the symbol can be revealed only in the concrete reality of the symbol, so can the creativity embodied in books, which Moses ibn Ezra called 'the sheaths of wisdom,' be manifested only via its material product.

Scholem's passion for collecting books and for bibliographical investigation had both a private and a public side. In the private

1 S.Y. Agnon, *Mi-'azmi el 'azmi*, Jerusalem–Tel Aviv, 1976, p. 276.
2 *Ibid.*

realm, Scholem possessed a strong, almost irrational passion to assemble a complete collection of books in all the broad areas connected to his research. His ardor first showed itself when, while still a boy, he sold his collection of children's books to an antiquarian dealer in Berlin and started buying books in the fields of history, mathematics and literature. At age fourteen his emergent Jewish consciousness sent him searching for texts, and he began buying books on Jewish subjects. When he plunged into the study of kabbalistic literature, he embarked with unbounded fervor upon a systematic quest to acquire and assemble every known text, source and secondary study on Jewish mysticism.

Scholem brought two thousand books with him when he immigrated to Palestine, six hundred of them on the Kabbala. From both his memoirs and several of his spoken remarks, it is evident that Jerusalem captivated him first and foremost by virtue of the abundance of books to be had there. Post–World War One Jerusalem was 'awash' in old Hebrew books: the booksellers were not expert in the nature or value of their wares, money was scarce, and few as yet took an interest in book collecting. Immediately upon his arrival, Scholem began to scour all the bookshops of the Old City's Jewish Quarter and the Mea Shearim neighborhood. As he put it in his memoirs, while the National Library, located at the time in the Bnai Brith House, was his place of work, nearby Me'a She'arim was his 'playground.'[3]

Scholem was interested in works of all sorts, even seemingly worthless ones. The literary critic Dov Sadan once offered to give him a certain work on Jonathan Eybeschuetz, a controversial figure who figured prominently in Scholem's later research on the history of Sabbateanism. Scholem responded, 'I don't have ...'s book on Eybeschuetz, and if you wish to honor me with it, I am willing and ready to accept, for even such a book, filled as it is with fabrications, belongs in my library. It is nevertheless most interesting to see the responses of people of this sort.'[4]

3 *From Berlin to Jerusalem*, New York 1980, p. 168.
4 Dov Sadan Archives, Jewish National and University Library, No. 03086, n.d.

Scholem purchased his first book on Kabbala in Berlin in 1915. It was a copy of the *Zohar*, on whose title page he inscribed *Gershom Ish Shalom* (1915). Twenty-two years later, his home in Jerusalem contained an almost complete collection of kabbalistic sources, including multiple editions and impressions, and he had also amassed most of the scholarly studies on the subject published up to that time. In 1937 he printed *Quntres 'alu le-shalom* ('Come to Scholem'), a list of rare titles on Kabbala and Hasidism, eighty in Hebrew and thirty-one in other languages, which he considered essential to make his collection complete. Many years later, at the opening of an exhibition at the Jewish National and University Library, Scholem admitted that the publication of this list had been a serious mistake on his part, for it made the prices of the books soar, and every Judaica collector attempted to obtain them. He further confessed that the title suggested by S.Y. Agnon had so beguiled him with its word-play on the phrase *'alu le-shalom* ('go you up in peace,' Gen. 45:17) that he lost his head and proceeded with this rash act. His confession is revealing of Scholem's fascination with the richly allusive Hebrew language, which he pressed into the service of his ideas in a literary style without peer in Jewish scholarship. Some thirty years later this list of *desiderata* had shrunk considerably. Only six of the rare books he had not succeeded in acquiring are to be found in the National Library; the rest are apparently books that were never actually printed, but were noted mistakenly in old lists that Scholem consulted.

Scholem's collector's passion continued until the very end of his life; he purchased books even from his deathbed. He left a magnificent library of more than twenty thousand volumes, which he donated to the Jewish National and University Library while he was still alive. It is the most comprehensive collection in the world of books, pamphlets, broadsheets, and offprints in the field of Jewish mysticism.

II

Scholem's special relationship with books was manifested in the public realm not only in the penetrating bibliographical investigations

studded throughout his works, but also in his specifically bibliographical publications, in his ongoing relationship with the Jewish
National and University Library, and in several of the scholarly
projects he headed.

Characteristically, Scholem's expertise in Hebrew bibliography
was achieved systematically. He speaks in his memoirs of the
countless hours he spent in the magnificent library of Moses Marx
before his departure for Palestine, often spending entire nights
furthering his knowledge of Hebrew bibliography and typography.
Indeed, Scholem gained entry into the country on the strength of an
official letter of invitation sent by Samuel Hugo Bergmann, director
of the Jewish National Library (which had just been transferred to
the auspices of the nascent Hebrew University), to take up a fictitious
post as librarian. When Scholem arrived in 1923, he chose working
at the library over teaching mathematics at a teachers' seminary, for
at the library he would be dealing with books, and, as he wrote,
'almost everything about them interested me.'[5] From 1923 to 1927
he was head of the library's Hebraica and Judaica department, his
post financed at first by what was known as 'the schnorring fund'
(cash donations left by visiting tourists) and only later formally
established. Scholem threw himself into helping Bergmann build
a major institution — under trying circumstances and with no
funds, as he related in his reminiscences of Bergmann[6] — and he
energetically developed the most important part of the library, the
national section. In 1927 the library published a classification system
for Judaica developed and introduced by Scholem, adapting the
Dewey classification system to the special requirements of Judaica.
The 'Scholem system,' revised and updated, is used to this day at
the Jewish National and University Library; it has been adopted by
other libraries as well, and has been translated into English.

Kiryat Sefer (or *Kirjath Sepher*, as the title was then spelt), the
library's bibliographical quarterly and the oldest still-active Hebrew
journal, began to appear shortly after Scholem's appointment to the
library's board of directors. He was one of its major contributors,

5   *From Berlin to Jerusalem*, p. 163.
6   G. Scholem, *Iyyun*, XXVI (1976), pp. 59–61.

publishing articles about authors and works on Kabbala, both in print and in manuscript, as well as short reviews and bibliographical notes of astonishing erudition. He and the historian Ben-Zion Dinaburg (later Dinur) were also in charge of the book lists; in fact, Scholem wrote and prepared for publication most of the issues of *Kiryat Sefer* in its first three years. All of Scholem's early Hebrew-language articles and reviews, twenty-two in number, appeared in those early issues, each of them graced by a charming style. His catalogue of the kabbalistic manuscripts owned by the library, prepared with the aid of Issachar Joel, appeared in 1930; to this day it remains an unparalleled research tool.

III

Scholem's special relationship with the library did not end with the conclusion of his employment there and the beginning of his university teaching career, but lasted to the end of his life. He published scores of articles in *Kirjath Sepher*, was continuously involved in the library's projects and acquisitions, and assisted in the expansion of its collections. He saw the assembly of all the written records of Jewish culture in the National Library in Jerusalem as a way of ensuring Jewish continuity, and he devoted himself fervently to that goal. His crowning achievement in this respect was the sacred task he took upon himself of rescuing the collections of Hebrew and Jewish books confiscated by the Nazis. After the war, in the summer of 1946, Scholem set out for Europe as a representative of the Hebrew University. For five long and arduous months he gathered information about the fate of Jewish libraries, located concentrations of books in Germany, Czechoslovakia and Austria, examined their contents, and conducted complicated and sensitive negotiations in order to salvage them, under indescribably difficult conditions. For several years he supervised the rescue and transfer of some half-million books and hundreds of manuscripts, from Germany, Czechoslovakia, Poland and Austria, to the Jewish National and University Library and other libraries in Israel. The transfer of Scholem's own priceless library to the Jewish National and University Library immortalized his deep and enduring relationship to the library of the Jewish nation.

Two of Scholem's works are devoted entirely to bibliography. As early as 1927, he published his *Bibliographia Cabbalistica*, still the only bibliography in its field, containing 1,302 entries on Kabbala and a list of 273 editions of the *Zohar*, its addenda and commentaries. Scholem's own working copy is marked up with hundreds of additional handwritten entries. In 1928 he published an annotated bibliography of the literature of the Bratslav Hasidim as a fiftieth-birthday present for Martin Buber. This booklet, selected by Buber's friends as a most befitting gift, was enlivened with an apposite *gematria* for the year of the book's publication.[7]

IV

Scholem expressed both his love for Hebrew printed books and manuscripts and the great importance he attached to their systematic and scholarly treatment in a number of projects he initiated and supervised. He was one of the fathers of the Hebrew Bibliography Project housed in the Jewish National and University Library. For twenty-two years, from its inception in 1960, he sat at the head of the editorial board of this large-scale effort to investigate and record in detail every item of Hebrew printed matter. At the board's last meeting, Scholem commented that he had resigned from all his posts on various committees other than this, which he considered one of the most significant endeavors being carried out in the field of Judaic Studies.

Scholem also headed the committee supervising the Hebrew Palaeography Project. In 1965 an ambitious proposal was put forward to the Israel Academy of Sciences and Humanities to study all dated medieval Hebrew manuscripts, to gather information about their technical, technological and graphic features, and then to computerize all this data, in order to arrive at a typology of Hebrew manuscripts. Scholem was most enthusiastic in his support for the project, assisting at every step with his extraordinary combination of broad vision and concern for detail.

---

7 'Shenat *le-Martin Buber le-yom ha-yovel* lifrat,' i.e., [5]688 (= 1928). Scholem published addenda to this list in *Kirjath Sepher*, VI (1929).

He similarly supported another extensive project, the Institute of Microfilmed Hebrew Manuscripts, which was established in order to collect microfilms of all the Hebrew manuscripts in hundreds of collections around the world, identify and catalogue them. This project, more than any other, has made and will continue to make a lasting impression on the field of Judaic Studies. Twenty-five years before David Ben-Gurion, the first Prime Minister of Israel, initiated the establishment of this institute, Scholem wrote to Bialik: 'The requisite manuscripts ... must be photographed ... and assembled in a special collection under the aegis of the University Library, so that those which are not published will yet be available for all the generations to come.'[8]

Although Gershom Scholem is no longer with us, he has left us his magnificent library, the love invested in it, the magic with which he endowed it and the many comments he jotted in the margins of its books. Referring to his library in a letter to Agnon, Scholem cited a remark by the Baal Shem Tov, founder of Hasidism, that 'all a person's household items, his dwelling and his surroundings are filled with the sparks of his soul and are waiting to be lifted up.'[9]

Scholem's spirit hovers over his library; the sparks of his soul are hidden within it. He has left us and generations to come the challenge of raising them up.

---

8 *Devarim be-go*, p. 61.
9 Agnon Archives, Jewish National and University Library, No. 5:429. The remark by the Baal Shem Tov is quoted by his grandson, R. Moses Hayyim Ephraim of Sudylkow, in his *Degel mahane Ephraim*, Jerusalem 1963, p. 96. (I am indebted to Prof. Yehuda Liebes for this reference.)